# Mastering Financial Management

## Demystify finance and transform your financial skills of management

# Mastering Financial Management

Demystify finance and transform
your financial skills of management

Stephen Brookson

THOROGOOD

Published by

Thorogood Ltd

12-18 Grosvenor Gardens

London SW1W 0DH

0171 824 8257

A catalogue record for this book is available from the British Library

ISBN 1 85418 067 3 (Trade edition)

ISBN 1 85418 101 7

Printed in Great Britain by Ashford Colour Press

# The author

## Stephen Brookson

Stephen Brookson is Managing Director of his company, New City Consulting, which specialises in the provision of practical business development consultancy and training programmes.

He qualified as a Chartered Accountant in 1980 with Peat Marwick and after a period at Grandmet plc, he joined a leading organisation in the provision of training for chartered accountants in practice. During this time he gained extensive experience of writing, developing and presenting programmes on accountancy and taxation. He then joined Ernst & Young for a number of years as a consultant, leaving them to set up his own management and training consultancy business. He has presented numerous seminars and training events in both the public and private sectors, in the UK and overseas.

# Contents

Icons ................................................................................11

**Chapter 1: Finance makes the world go round** ...............................13

**Who this is for** ..............................................................14
    You are not alone ......................................................14

**Overview** .....................................................................15
    Other sources ...........................................................15
    Users and uses of financial information .................................16
    Financial versus management accounting ...............................17
    Name that accountant ...................................................18

**Rules governing accounting** ...................................................20
    Law .......................................................................20
    Accounting standards ...................................................20
    International dimension ..................................................24
    Big GAAP/Little GAAP ...................................................24

**Corporate financial health** ...................................................25
    Audits ...................................................................25
    Corporate reality .......................................................25

**SSAP 2** .......................................................................25
    1 Accruals (or matching) concept .......................................26
    2 Going concern ........................................................27
    3 Consistency ..........................................................27
    4 Prudence .............................................................28

**Basic accounts** ...............................................................28
    Profit and loss account .................................................29

**Balance sheet** ................................................................34
    The two business cycles .................................................35
    Fixed assets ............................................................35
    Cost .....................................................................36
    Revaluations ...........................................................36

Depreciation ..................................................................................38

Depreciation method...........................................................................40

Notes to accounts ............................................................................43

**Current assets and current liabilities** ...............................................44

Current assets ................................................................................44

Working capital example ...................................................................46

Current liabilities ............................................................................48

Ratio analysis ................................................................................48

Other current liabilities ....................................................................50

Critical issues ................................................................................50

**Long-term liabilities** ....................................................................51

Creditors due after more than one year ...............................................51

Historical cost ................................................................................51

Balance sheet summary ....................................................................52

**Other side of the balance sheet**......................................................52


**Chapter 2: Analysing performance** .................................................55

**Interpreting accounts using ratio analysis** ......................................56

Introduction ..................................................................................56

Return on capital employed (ROCE) ....................................................56

Tree of ratios ................................................................................58

**Profitability measures** .................................................................59

Earnings per share (EPS) ..................................................................60

**Balance sheet measures** ...............................................................61

Asset turnover ...............................................................................61

Fixed asset turnover ........................................................................61

Debtor days...................................................................................62

Stock days....................................................................................63

Creditor days ................................................................................63

Current ratio .................................................................................63

Quick ratio ...................................................................................64

Stock to net assets .........................................................................65

Stock turnover ...............................................................................65

**Finance ratios** ...................................................................................66

    Gearing/borrowing ratio .................................................66

    Interest cover ....................................................................67

**Match the business with ratios** .........................................67

**Proforma ratios** ....................................................................69

**Match the business with ratios:** *solution*.........................70

**Practical working capital management** .............................71

    Debtors................................................................................71

    Stock ..................................................................................72

    Creditors ............................................................................73

**Detailed case study** ..............................................................73

    Analysis .............................................................................73

    Helpful hints ....................................................................74

    Profit and loss account analysis ...................................76

    Balance sheet analysis ...................................................77

    A calculation ....................................................................83

    Break-even ........................................................................84


**Chapter 3:  External analysis**..............................................85

**A source of intelligence** ......................................................86

    News stories .....................................................................86

    Back page ..........................................................................86

    Major quoted companies ................................................87

    FTSE 100.............................................................................87

    Share prices.......................................................................87

    FTSE movements...............................................................88

    Share data..........................................................................88

    Market capitalisation ......................................................89

    Price earnings – computation.........................................89

    Price earnings – comparison...........................................90

    Price earnings – valuation tool......................................91

    Yield gross ........................................................................92

    Gilts and interest rates ..................................................93

## Chapter 4:  Review of accounting principles .................................................. 95

**Introduction** ................................................................. 96

**Fixed assets and depreciation** ................................................. 96

Carrying cost ............................................................... 96

Depreciation period ........................................................ 97

Residual value ............................................................. 98

Depreciation methods ....................................................... 98

Straight line depreciation ................................................. 99

Production or use method ................................................... 99

Accelerated depreciation methods ........................................... 100

Depreciation for tax purposes .............................................. 100

Expenditure eligible for allowances ........................................ 101

Rates of capital allowances ................................................ 101

Property ................................................................... 102

**Long-term liabilities** ....................................................... 102

Long-term debt ............................................................. 103

Long-term leases ........................................................... 103

Leasing .................................................................... 105

Sale and leaseback ......................................................... 110

Other long-term debt ....................................................... 110

Discounts, premiums and cash flow .......................................... 112

Deep discounts ............................................................. 113

Sinking funds .............................................................. 113

Warrants ................................................................... 113

Notes, loan notes and commercial paper ..................................... 114

Bonds ...................................................................... 114

Mezzanine finance .......................................................... 114

Provisions and estimated liabilities ....................................... 114

Provisions ................................................................. 115

Pensions ................................................................... 115

Commitments ................................................................ 116

Contingent liabilities ..................................................... 116

**Owners' equity in companies** ................................................. 117

Ordinary shares: basic concepts.......................................117

Preference shares: basic concepts ....................................118

Ordinary shares: technical terms .....................................119

Share premium account ..................................................119

Stock dividend ...............................................................120

Scrip or bonus issue ......................................................120

Share splits ..................................................................120

Rights issue .................................................................121

Share options................................................................121

Retained earnings..........................................................121

Revaluation reserve........................................................122

Other reserves ..............................................................122

**Notes to the accounts** ......................................................122

Overview .....................................................................122

Annual report and accounts ............................................123

Directors' report ...........................................................124

Notes to the accounts ....................................................124

Stock valuation .............................................................126

Depreciation and amortisation charge ...............................126

Changes in accounting policy ..........................................127

Leases .........................................................................127

Contingent liabilities......................................................128

Debt structure ..............................................................128

Equity structure ............................................................129

Contractual liabilities ....................................................129

Segmental and geographical analysis ...............................130

Other types of notes to the accounts ...............................130

**GAAP mechanism** ............................................................130

Generally Accepted Accounting Principles..........................130

Organisations that influence GAAP ...................................131

**Auditing principles** .........................................................132

Role of the auditor – accounting firms and services ...........132

Audited financial statements ...........................................133

Limitations of the auditing process ................................................134

The audit report ..............................................................................135

Basic elements ...............................................................................136

Statements of responsibility ..........................................................137

Expression of opinion .....................................................................137

Unqualified opinion ........................................................................138

Qualified opinion ............................................................................138

Limitations of audit scope .............................................................140

Disclaimer of opinion .....................................................................140

Adverse opinion ..............................................................................141

Except for disagreement..................................................................141

Fundamental uncertainty ...............................................................141

Directors' responsibilities ..............................................................142

Unaudited financial statements......................................................142

## Chapter 5:  Budgeting and management accounting...............................145

**Budgeting** ..........................................................................................146

Introduction  ..................................................................................146

Budgeting in general.......................................................................147

Control ............................................................................................147

Reward ............................................................................................148

Communication  ..............................................................................148

Long and short-term planning  .......................................................148

Budget problems..............................................................................150

Period for the budget  .....................................................................150

Budget administration .....................................................................150

**Setting a budget**.................................................................................152

Critical factor..................................................................................152

Sales budget  ..................................................................................153

Other budgets  ................................................................................153

Negotiation .....................................................................................153

Co-ordination and review ................................................................154

Final acceptance..............................................................................154

**Reviewing a budget**..................................................................155

　Inherent uncertainty ........................................................155

　Three level budgets ..........................................................156

　Probability analysis ..........................................................157

　Sensitivity analysis ..........................................................158

**Zero-based budgeting** ........................................................159

　Purpose of zero-based budgeting (ZBB) ..........................159

　The principle of ZBB ........................................................160

　Advantages of ZBB ..........................................................161

　Disadvantages of ZBB ......................................................162

　Budgeting behaviour in organisations ..............................162

　Motivation........................................................................162

　Your business ..................................................................163

　Cash budgeting ..............................................................163

**Monitoring a budget** ..........................................................168

　Definition and purposes of budgetary control ..................168

　Budget realism ................................................................169

　Control limits..................................................................169

　Comparing actual and budget ..........................................170

　Marginal or total costing ................................................170

**Management accounting** ....................................................171

　Responsibility and variances – an improvement

　on the common-sense approach ......................................171

　A more realistic standard ................................................172

　Planning and operational variances ................................173

　Reasons for variances occurring ....................................173

　Controllable and uncontrollable costs.............................174

　When to investigate variances ........................................174

**Better management accounting** ........................................175

　Balanced business scorecard............................................180

**Chapter 6: Costs**.................................................................................183

**Introduction**...................................................................................184

**Break-even**......................................................................................185

    Break-even charts.......................................................................185

    Bringing businesses to life ...........................................................187

    Outsourcing ..............................................................................187

    Finance out ..............................................................................188

    Risk and reward .........................................................................188

    Break-even points .......................................................................189

    Life is not all straight lines ...........................................................190

**Building up costs** ..............................................................................192

    Menu pricing .............................................................................193

    Total costing pitfalls ....................................................................194

    Overheads ...............................................................................195

    Mark-up and margin ....................................................................196

    Marginal versus total costing .........................................................198

    Comprehensive example ...............................................................199

    Direct and indirect costs ..............................................................201

    Business cost generalisations .........................................................203

    Product profitability ....................................................................203

    Typical allocations .....................................................................204

    Typical conclusions .....................................................................206

    New good, old bad? ....................................................................207

    Activity based costing ..................................................................207

    Drawbacks to ABC ......................................................................208

**Decision-making**...............................................................................209

    Backwards and forwards...............................................................209

    Inside and outside .....................................................................210

    Brave new world ........................................................................211

    Winds of change ........................................................................211

    Decision time – case study ............................................................212

    Look forward ............................................................................213

**Golden rules for decisions** ...................................................................215

Sunk costs ..................................................................215

Relevant costs ............................................................215

Incremental or opportunity .......................................215

A worthwhile opportunity? .........................................217

If the figures don't fit ..............................................220

Sensitivity analysis ....................................................220

Make or buy decisions ...............................................221

Buy ............................................................................221

Does anyone get it right? ..........................................222

A good move? ............................................................223

**Organisational decision flaws** ...................................224

Profit centres ............................................................224

Play make-believe ......................................................225

Bend the rules to suit ...............................................226

Transfer prices ..........................................................227

The wasted debate ....................................................228

Profit centre decay ....................................................228

Directors as referees .................................................229

Profit centre disaster 1 .............................................229

Profit centre disaster 2 .............................................231

One inevitable conclusion ..........................................232

Payment in paper clips, please ..................................233

**Pros and cons of profit centres** .................................233

Terminal decay ..........................................................234

**Chapter 7: Computing future decisions** .......................235

**Dealing with the future** .............................................236

A more scientific approach ........................................236

Conventions ...............................................................237

**Accounting rate of return** ..........................................237

An alternative scenario .............................................238

**Payback period** ..........................................................239

Payback norms ..........................................................239

A cash flow measure? ....................................................................240

Single independent project...............................................................240

Mutually exclusive projects.............................................................241

**Time value of money**...................................................................241

Present values ............................................................................241

Discounting ................................................................................242

Future values, or compounding .....................................................243

Inflation plays no part ..................................................................243

**Discounted cash flow** ................................................................244

Net present value ........................................................................245

Effect of discount rate..................................................................245

Internal rate of return ..................................................................246

IRR and NPV together ...................................................................246

**Summary of criteria** ..................................................................247

**Interest rate**.............................................................................247

Marginal ....................................................................................248

Weighted....................................................................................248

Hurdle or premium ......................................................................249

**Time scale** ...............................................................................250

**Accuracy** .................................................................................251

Final pleas.................................................................................251

**Learning cycle** ..........................................................................252

Plan, do, review, think – or do we? ................................................253

**Comprehensive example** ...........................................................254

Solution ....................................................................................254

**Final thoughts** ..........................................................................257

# Icons

Throughout the Masters in Management series of books you will see references and symbols in the margins. These are designed for ease of use and quick reference directing you quickly to key features of the text. The symbols used are:

We would encourage you to use this book as a workbook, writing notes and comments in the margin as they occur. In this way we hope that you will benefit from the practical guidance and advice which this book provides.

# Finance makes
# the world go round

# Chapter 1

# Who this is for

This book is aimed at people who have got to a certain time and position in their working life, but who now find that something is missing. You may be particularly talented at marketing, engineering or information technology. Yet when it comes to that monthly board meeting to discuss your department's results you can't help but feel that you've missed out on something. You don't seem to speak the same language as the other people, and yet you know that *you* are the one that understands the business far better than they do. So why do they have the figures and the answers? Surely that's something that you should be doing? If only you had the confidence, and a little understanding of the basics, you feel that you would be able to challenge what they say – and help to build a more prosperous business in the future.

## You are not alone

In my travels of trying to bring financial learning to sensible managers like you a few simple corporate truths have struck me.

Firstly, it is quite staggering how much resource is spent on training and development at the less tangible end of the spectrum. Just count how many effective time management, assertiveness and team building programmes you have been on in your lifetime. Now count how many effective finance programmes you have attended.

Secondly, consider my 'Jekyll and Hyde' theory to financial competence. You probably manage a large budget, be it thousands or millions. When you walk in the office door at nine o'clock in the morning you are all bristling efficiency and calm competence. You sit down and digest columns of figures, making far-reaching decisions in the twinkling of an eye. Could you be the same person who, barely an hour before, left home – where the finances are in total chaos? When did you last reconcile your personal bank account? Do you have a family cash flow forecast, profit and loss account and balance sheet? Were you, too, wrongly sold an endowment mortgage and a personal pension? Have you made a will? Have you bed and breakfasted your windfall shares – or do you like paying tax needlessly? Do you have any idea about any of the financial products you have bought recently? No, of course you don't – you're just like most other people in this country! So what on earth makes you think that you are a financially fit person to lead your business into a profitable future?

Thirdly, you are bright, learn quickly, but really 'don't know what you don't know' about finance.

So, you are, in some respects, a bluffer. You have managed to get to where you are today in spite of your pretty appalling financial competence. Sound familiar?

# Overview

One of the things that you have probably already come across is the sheer number and volume of books and products available to help people like you in this situation. So why is this book different?

## Other sources

For example, there are brilliant books around on creative accounting, costing and pricing, management accounting, personal financial planning and so on – and I will suggest a list of them that you might like to delve into if you are interested in learning more. I am not trying to write one book that replaces all the others – that simply wouldn't be feasible. Instead I am trying to provide you with a text of 'First Call', something that will give you an overall context and set of signposts to help you navigate through the jungle of financial jargon.

This book will give you the confidence and impetus to go back to work and ask more from the scorekeepers who inhabit the accounts department.

Some commentators say that there are really only two key business functions: marketing and finance. I would agree, but add that there is little or no point in marketing something that isn't going to make any money in the first place. So in my book, finance is the critical business skill to possess before you can set course for a successful business career.

However, the nature of financial expertise within an organisation has changed forever. Simple things such as advances in IT have all ensured that the organisation has passed down budgetary and financial responsibility. These are all trends that are here to stay.

## Users and uses of financial information

Let's think awhile about just exactly who is interested in a set of financial statements. In other words, who are the users and what are the uses of financial information – and where are you.

**Users and uses of financial statements**

| User | Reason |
|---|---|
| Shareholder | Value of investment |
| Management | Business performance |
| Customer | Solidity of business |
| Supplier | Credit worthiness |
| Tax authorities | Profitability and tax paid |
| Competitors | Relative performance |
| Broker/analyst | Recommendation to buy/sell |
| Employee | Security of employment/profit share |

Just where are you in this list? Your perspective on finance will of course determine just what you are looking for from business financial information.

Probably the most important 'split' within the world of financial information lies between the inward looking world of internal management information, as opposed to the external focused world of financial accounting and reporting.

*Key Question*

## Financial versus management accounting

How do we define management and financial accounting? What are the differences, and how will we cover them in this book? Essentially we will examine the fundamentals of financial accounting first. In later chapters we will go on to look at how the internal management accounting function supports the overall business in its struggle to meet its financial targets.

*Key Question*

Typically, however, you are likely to encounter the two branches as described below.

*Key Management Concept*

### Financial versus management accounting

| | Financial Accounting | Management Accounting |
|---|---|---|
| **Governed by** | Company Law | Needs of managers |
| **Users** | External | Internal |
| **Time Period** | One year | As appropriate |
| **Coverage** | Company/group | Divisions/sub-group |
| **Emphasis** | Accuracy | Speed |
| **Criteria** | Objective Verifiable | Useful Understandable |
| **Unit of account** | Money | Money, units |
| **Nature of data** | Somewhat technical | Used by non-accountants |

## Name that accountant

Since we have already started to spread the accounting 'net' to financial and management accounts, we might as well play 'Name that accountant' now. How many different types of UK accountant can you name? What does each do, where are you most likely to encounter them in your organisation and what do they do in your organisation?

The UK has the dubious statistic of having one of the highest accountant-to-population ratios in the world. Would that surprise you? One more fact is that we in this country have a very fragmented set of accounting professional bodies. This is a source of great despair to some industry insiders and our overseas colleagues, who cannot understand why we are not all united under one umbrella (as is the Certified Public Accountant qualification in the USA).

Currently we have Chartered (ACA/CA/ACAI), Certified (ACCA), Management (CIMA), Public Sector (CIPFA), Technician (AAT) and so on. In the chapter on technical matters there is a more thorough review of the various accounting bodies and the role that they all play in setting standards.

# Rules governing accounting

For those of you who think that accounting is black and white, you are in for a shock. Accounting is, like many of its exponents, various shades of grey. How have we got ourselves into this sort of position? In order to understand how, we need to look at the rules that govern our accounting environment. We accountants live in a magnificent structure supported by the twin pillars of Statute and Self-regulation.

## Law

The primary legislation we work under is laid out by the Companies Acts. We have been influenced, like many areas of UK law has recently, by the need to implement EC Directives. We have indeed been a good EC neighbour in these matters. I like to think of the Companies Acts as the 'skeleton' of corporate reporting: it tells you the basic rules, framework, rights and responsibilities, outlines, duties and so on. What it does not tell you about are the accounting subtleties and nuances.

## Accounting standards

The subtleties are, instead, covered in a separate set of accounting 'law', called accounting standards. Actually the correct term is GAAP, or Generally Accepted Accounting Practice. GAAP deals with the accounting nuances, or the areas of subjectivity, nuance and debates which are simply not addressed by the Companies Acts.

Just as the Companies Acts I likened to the corporate reporting 'skeleton', so GAAP is the flesh on that skeleton that gives the whole construction life!

Just thinking about the first two words – Generally Accepted – should give you a clue that we are in fact an example of a self-regulatory organisation (SRO) setting our own rules.

GAAP started around the beginning of the 1970s, when each pronouncement was known at the time as a SSAP, or Statement of Standard Accounting Practice. We managed to get up to the mid twenties (with a few casualties) by 1991, when we rebadged the SSAP and launched it as the new updated FRS, or Financial Reporting Standard. As of early 1998 we have reached the dizzy heights of FRS 10, having therefore issued about one and a half FRSs each year. This has recently made the 'financial engineering' of corporate accounts extremely difficult, and there is currently considerable ill will about the complexity and frequency of FRSs.

What follows is a list and title of the current GAAP statements. Over the years the following statements have been issued (and in some cases withdrawn).

*Key Management Concept*

| SSAP | NARRATIVE |
|------|-----------|
| **1** | Accounting for Associated Companies |
| **2** | Disclosure of Accounting Policies/Fundamental Accounting Principals |
| **3** | Earnings Per Share |
| **4** | Accounting for Government Grants |
| **5** | Accounting for Value Added Tax |
| **8** | Taxation under the Imputation System |
| **9** | Accounting for Stocks and Long-Term Contracts |
| **12** | Accounting for Depreciation |
| **13** | Accounting for Research and Development |
| **15** | Accounting for Deferred Tax |
| **17** | Accounting for Post Balance Sheet Events |
| **18** | Accounting for Contingencies |
| **19** | Accounting for Investment Properties |
| **20** | Foreign Currency Translation |
| **21** | Accounting for Leases and Hire Purchase Contracts |
| **22** | Accounting for Goodwill |
| **24** | Accounting for Pension Costs |
| **25** | Segmental Reporting |

| FRS | NARRATIVE |
|-----|-----------|
| **1** | Cash Flow Statements |
| **2** | Accounting for Subsidiary Undertakings |
| **3** | Reporting Financial Performance |
| **4** | Capital Instruments |
| **5** | Reporting the Substance of Transactions |
| **6** | Acquisitions and Mergers |
| **7** | Fair Values in Acquisition Accounting |
| **8** | Related Party Disclosures |
| **9** | Associates and Joint Ventures |
| **10** | Goodwill and Intangible Assets |

You can see that GAAP has addressed the main accounting and scorekeeping issues – the earlier ones fixed the most immediate problems. Nowadays FRSs tend to be more complex overall and longer in word, such are the issues that they tend to address.

What really prompted the change to the FRS regime was the incidence of corporate failure in the late 1980s and early 1990s, with all of the failed companies having clean audit reports and showing no external signs of financial distress. Just what were accountants doing wrong, it was being asked? Well, as it turned out, it wasn't all our fault, but a little stable cleaning did not go amiss.

## International dimension

In contrast with equivalent mechanisms in other countries, we line up with the rest of the English speaking world. Polar opposites are the French, with their Napoleonic codified system to such a degree that all companies have the same account numbers. Somewhere in between lie other countries.

What results is enormous difficulty in knowing which accounting 'language' is correct. For example a French company recently announced a profit of several billion francs, but when the results had been translated into US GAAP the profit turned in to a loss of twenty billion francs. Same sales, same cash generated, same assets – different language! We are winning the international war for two reasons – English as a language, and the fact that we and the USA have the most developed stock markets and hence corporate reports.

In summary, as a UK accountant I will go to war to defend my 'Subjective and Flexible' accounting regime that I treasure so much. I reject any attempt to go down the alternative 'Objective and Inflexible' route so beloved by European accountants. So much for a unified Europe!

## Big GAAP/Little GAAP

Currently there is a debate on the need for smaller businesses to follow the whole majesty of UK GAAP in its entirety. Frankly, for the majority of UK companies GAAP is pretty irrelevant, and is a massive burden. Why, it is being argued, can we not have a simplified set of GAAP specifically for the smaller business?

This Big GAAP versus Little GAAP debate has philosophical difficulties for certain accountants who simply say that size doesn't matter, and all businesses should be subject to the same rules. Watch this space.

# Corporate financial health

## Audits

We will examine audits and auditors in more detail later. The important thing to acknowledge here is that they do not prepare accounts. A quick look at the 'Directors' responsibility' statement in the accounts should be sufficient to convince you that all they do is to provide the 'true and fair' certificate to the accounts already prepared by the directors. Nothing more.

Auditors are constantly struggling to tell the public what they do and what they don't do, and they often refer to this as the 'public perception gap'.

## Corporate reality

We must always appreciate the fundamental concept of company, with ownership separate to the business itself. This concept was recognised in law in the last century, and ever since then there has been a need to regulate and control the potential abuse that is so prevalent with limited liability.

# SSAP 2

In a later chapter we will look at some key GAAP statements in more detail. All we need to do now is to examine SSAP 2, since all subsequent GAAP is in reality a follow on from SSAP 2.

So why wasn't it SSAP 1, then, if it is actually that important? Well it got pipped at the post by something more technical in nature. Instead the most important SSAP of all, and the most forgotten of all, languishes in the anonymous title of SSAP 2 on 'Disclosure of Accounting Policies'. Actually it contains just about the closest thing we have in the UK to a conceptual framework for accounting, and SSAP 2 is often known therefore as 'Fundamental Accounting Concepts'.

*Action Checklist*

Read and learn these four well known sayings. Not only do the words keep on cropping up in all things financial, they are critical to the way we prepare accounts in the UK. Test out your accountant the next time you see them with the friendly grenade 'Just remind me what the four fundamental accounting principles are'.

# 1   Accruals (or matching) concept

*Key Learning Point*

All UK accounts, including the public sector, are prepared using the accruals or matching concept. That is to say accounts contain income and expenditure on an arising basis. The arising basis means that something is counted as a cost in an accounting period if the item has been consumed – never mind that it might not have been paid for. Similarly income is scored if it has been earned, never mind that it has not yet been received.

The accruals basis is therefore the opposite of the cash basis. We do not produce accounts based on whether cash has actually been paid or received – we do not think that gives a fair picture.

It's quite simple, really, and quite logical. The big drawback is that the profit shown may bear little resemblance to the cash collected. We have become a nation driven by the profit and loss account, often blissfully unaware of the true cash situation within a business until it's too late.

## 2   Going concern

The going concern principle simply states that in preparing accounts we assume that the business will still be trading into the future. Whilst this sounds straightforward, the alternative is too dreadful to contemplate.

Consider your own business and the fixed assets (plant and machinery, cars, computers and so on) that it owns. What would be the actual market value of those assets should you go out of business (the opposite of the going concern basis)? All those assets would be worth considerably less than what they were being shown as in the balance sheet; so should we show them at their break-up value? No, we always assume a going concern, otherwise we will never be able to measure a business fairly.

Going concern is simply an assumption we need to make before we can prepare meaningful financial statements.

## 3   Consistency

This really defines itself – all accounts must be prepared on a consistent basis. That is to say the accounting policies and procedures should not change from year to year. Should they have to change, then the change must be clearly flagged-up and its effect on the financial statements quantified. Cynically, people will only change the way they scorekeep if there is a reason to do so – such as increased profit, a better balance sheet and so on.

Consistency is a relatively simple concept to explain, but harder to police and enforce.

## 4    Prudence

This is the accountant's clove of garlic to the vampire of a finance director. It is the accountants' most important accounting principle, and is etched on their hearts at qualification.

All financial statements should be prudent (conservative is the US equivalent word). This means that profits should not be overstated, and costs should never be understated. Imagine how well that might go down with a plc board of directors under pressure to produce ever-increasing profits!

It is prudence that really gives rise to all the main accounting debates, and by nature many of the answers have to rely on subjectivity, as we have already discussed.

## Basic accounts

We will now look at the three key financial statements – profit and loss account, balance sheet and cash flow. We will focus on the first two to start with, then the third in a later section.

Adherence to the accruals principle (good) means that the cash perspective is lost (bad) and we spend time 'unscrambling' the accrual statements to get tangible real cash flows. This has always been the problem and bane of most businesses' – or to put it in the rather trite but effective phrase, 'profits are vanity, cash is sanity'.

## Profit and loss account

The key concepts are that the profit and loss account contains income and expenditure on an accruals basis. It contains all the 'ins less outs', or items of a revenue (as opposed to a capital) nature.

It is useful to look at the accounting period, and the relevance of the accounting date (if not historically overtaken by other events). For example, the figures we will be looking at shortly are from a high street fashion retailer whose accounting period is the end of January. What is happening at the end of January in high street retailing – sales just over, lots of cash, low stock levels. Sounds like a good time to have an accounting period end, doesn't it? Stock levels, seasonality, convenience all play their part in this decision.

Here are the main headings to the profit and loss account, with description and key points of each. Read through the text below in conjunction with the following figures:

**FASHION RETAILER PLC**

*Profit and Loss Account*

|  | 1998 | 1997 |
|---|---|---|
| **Turnover** | 980 | 800 |
| Cost of Sales | 655 | 550 |
| **Gross profit** | 325 | 250 |
| Distribution costs | 110 | 100 |
| Administrative expenses | 60 | 50 |
| **Operating profit** | 155 | 100 |
| Other income | 10 | 30 |
| **Profit before interest** | 165 | 130 |
| Interest receivable | 15 | 15 |
| **Profit before taxation** | 180 | 145 |
| Taxation payable | 54 | 44 |
| **Profit for the year** | 126 | 102 |
| Dividends | 60 | 45 |
| **Retained profit for the year** | 66 | 57 |

# FASHION RETAILER PLC

*Balance Sheets*

| | | 1998 | 1997 |
|---|---|---|---|
| | | £ | £ |
| **Fixed Assets** | | | |
| Tangible assets | | 160 | 145 |
| **Current Assets** | | | |
| Stocks | | 129 | 94 |
| Debtors | | 240 | 185 |
| Cash in hand | | 175 | 180 |
| | *Total* | 544 | 459 |
| **Creditors due within one year** | | | |
| Trade and other creditors | | 65 | 62 |
| Taxation | | 54 | 44 |
| Other creditors | | 85 | 80 |
| Proposed dividend | | 60 | 45 |
| | *Total* | 264 | 231 |
| | *Net Current Assets* | 280 | 229 |
| **Creditors due after one year** | | 10 | 10 |
| | *Net worth* | 430 | 364 |
| | | | |
| **Capital and Reserves** | | | |
| Called-up share capital | | 40 | 40 |
| Other reserves | | 24 | 24 |
| Profit and loss account | | 366 | 300 |
| | *Total* | 430 | 364 |

## FASHION RETAILER PLC

| *Cash Flow Analysis* | | 1998 | 1997 |
|---|---|---|---|
| **Operating profit** | 155 | | |
| **Depreciation** | 20 | | |
| Increase in stocks | (35) | | |
| Increase in debtors | (55) | | |
| Decrease in creditors | 8 | | |
| | | 93 | 69 |
| **Returns on investment & servicing of finance** | | | |
| Interest received | | 15 | 12 |
| Other income | | 10 | 30 |
| **Taxation** | | | |
| Corporation tax paid | | (44) | (21) |
| **Capital expenditure and financial investment** | | | |
| Purchase of fixed assets | | (35) | (44) |
| **Acquisitions and disposals** | | | |
| Sale of subsidiary | | 1 | 45 |
| **Equity dividends paid** | | (45) | (38) |
| | | (5) | 53 |
| Opening cash balance | 180 | | 127 |
| Closing cash balance | 175 | | 180 |
| *Movement in cash balances* | | (5) | 53 |

### Sales

The first line in a profit and loss account has to do with the overall volume of activity, and is called either sales, income, fees billed or turnover. All exclude VAT.

### Costs of sales

Costs are generally taken off in two chunks. The first one is called cost of sales, and is above the line of gross profit. The other is deducted below gross profit in arriving at the net profit. What goes where, and what are the conventions and the unwritten rules?

If you mentioned such words as fixed, variable, direct and indirect costs, then you won't be a million miles away, but we'll discuss those later. They are all ways of classifying costs in two different, and additionally informative, perspectives. For the moment, however, they are not relevant.

Cost of goods sold (or COGS) or cost of sales – what does it include generally? It includes all the costs expended to make or produce the product or service that is being sold. Those costs can include staff, premises and materials costs. There is a grey area as to some costs such as distribution and marketing – typically they are not cost of sales, but some businesses treat them as such.

Gross is therefore a 'factory' result, whatever your factory might be or look like.

A typical range of gross margins could be between 7% and 80%, or Sainsbury to Microsoft. What type of business is likely to be at each end of the feasible spectrum? It all really depends on whether the business under review is high or low margin, high or low capital intensive, manufacturing or service. There is no such thing as absolutely good or bad (a concept we shall keep repeating throughout, especially when we get to the vexed area of ratio analysis), it is really more simply a matter of what you would expect for that business versus the actual outcome observed. Gross income is actually the most important sign of life for a business. When the gross starts disappearing, times are hard.

## Other costs

Other costs are broadly categorised into distribution and administration. In effect by the time these costs have been deducted, all the business' costs must have been dealt with. All typical ongoing business costs must therefore be shown as COGS or as other costs. As mentioned earlier there are grey areas of classification. Beware of reading too much into comparing gross/net between competitors who classify differently; typical examples of this confusion are distribution costs.

## Net Profit

A typical range of net margins is between 0% and 10%. Nobody actually sets out to make 0%, but it happens – and if the cash is still coming in then there is every reason to keep going. Net profit is effectively the end of the 'first half' of the profit and loss account, and is the part that reflects the true trading performance of the business. The rest of the profit and loss account does of course contain revenue and income, but not necessarily related to trading performance.

## Below net profit

What happens below the net or operating line? These are not core activities directly linked to operating performance, and are therefore not first line indicators. Nevertheless they will be expenses that the business clearly has to bear, in one form or other. Typical items are exceptionals, interest in or out, other income, taxation and dividends.

At the bottom line of the profit and loss account we see the concept of retained earnings. These retained earnings are the profit kept behind that make a business grow. **One key learning point is that the amount of profit, after everything else, will be the amount of the increase in the balance sheet**. Sometimes in a large company this simple accounting truth is obscured by technical shuffling, but for most businesses will be true. What we don't know is exactly where the additional profit will be: hopefully in a first-class asset such as cash, and not in a non-liquid item such as stock.

For a plc broadly the profit before tax gets split three ways. One third goes to the tax man (corporate tax rate is about 30%), one third to shareholders by way of dividend, and the final one third gets kept in the business.

### Summary

All businesses follow the same broad rules, but each will vary according to the industry and chosen accounting peculiarities of that industry.

One important measure of a profit and loss account is to express each line as a percentage of sales for that year. In doing this we gain a feel for the relationships within the business, and the technique is almost compulsory in financial analysis.

## Balance sheet

The key concept of a balance sheet is that it is a snapshot of a business assets less liabilities, or items of a capital (not revenue) nature. It is in essence a photograph taken of the whole business at midnight on the date of the end of the accounting period. This photograph is developed, and all the 'owns less owes' are then added up to give the balance sheet.

All assets and liabilities are identified, then put into the balance sheet according to the accounting convention called historic cost. That is, things are shown at their original historic cost to the business. There are certain exceptions to this which we will examine later: revalued amounts for certain assets and depreciation for assets which are being consumed within the essential business fabric.

Items are then categorised according to the laid down format: fixed assets, current assets, current liabilities, long-term liabilities.

## The two business cycles

The theory is that all businesses have two cycles: the capital investment cycle and the operating cycle. The latter is straightforward – goods and services are bought in order to sell goods and services. The operating cycle therefore contains such things that are consumed/rotated within the business simply by virtue of being in business.

The capital investment cycle, on the other hand, is a measure of how much is invested in the capital infrastructure in order that a business may carry out its operating cycle. Things here include all the classic fixed assets. You should note the implication here that manufacturing businesses tend to have high fixed assets (manufacturing plant, machines, equipment, warehouses and so on) and are capital intensive; whilst service businesses have low fixed assets (computers, equipment and perhaps company cars) and are not capital intensive.

## Fixed assets

Fixed assets are essentially those assets needed for the business to be able to trade. They are not assets that are bought and sold as part of trading or operating activities. There is a generally accepted distinction between the capital investment cycle and operating cycle.

A key point to note when examining fixed assets in a business is their value shown in the accounts, the depreciation provided, and hence the net book value. The concept of depreciation is really no more than accruals at work – depreciation writes off the cost of the asset being consumed (less any anticipated residual value, often assumed to be nil) over its effective useful life.

## Cost

Starting with the fundamental principle of UK accounts, all items should be shown at 'cost'. Cost will, of course, mean what the business paid in order to acquire that asset – but in some cases it may not. UK accounting allows specifically for one type of asset to be included at something other than cost.

Just thinking through the sorts of assets in a balance sheet, to show current assets at cost is entirely fair, since being current assets they must by definition convert into cash within a year.

Looking further afield to fixed assets, to show them at cost less depreciation provided to date seems fair as well, since the vast majority of fixed assets will fall in value as soon as they are brought into use (although, as discussed later, depreciation is not designed to show assets at second-hand value, nor is it there to provide a fund for replacement).

So how about cost – what do we put into the financial statements in the first place? The place to look for help is under the **Notes to the Accounts** in an Annual Report and Accounts, where note 1 (usually) says that 'The accounts are prepared under the historic cost convention, as modified by the revaluation of certain assets (land and buildings)'. Therefore the only exception to 'what we paid' for an asset as its cost is when we use a revalued amount. Note that almost all assets fall in value during their usage period, and this fall to some extent is reflected by the depreciation charge. So the only time we should be considering revaluation of certain assets is when they increase in value.

## Revaluations

What are these assets likely to be, that increase in value? Typically, for most businesses, they are going to be land and buildings of some form or other. For the moment let us just assume that since property generally increases in value (except for the last ten years, perhaps !) then putting a bigger (revalued) amount into the accounts will look impressive to readers – so we do it.

Where land and buildings can be shown to have appreciated in value, this appreciation can be shown in the accounts of the business. This adjustment will increase the 'cost' of the asset in the fixed asset section and so now the balance sheet doesn't balance. What is needed is an entry (equal to the amount by which the asset has been revalued upwards) on the share capital and reserves side of the balance sheet, but what do we call it, and where does it go ? It isn't share capital, it isn't a profit (because it hasn't yet been sold), and it isn't any other type of technical reserve that we've come across so far. The solution is that we invent a category called 'revaluation reserve'. This is what we refer to as a 'non-distributable' reserve; we are sitting on a surplus or potential profit, but the gain can only be distributed to shareholders as and when it has been realised. After all, the value of the land and building could go down before the business had time to sell it.

Here is an example of a business that is holding land at original cost of £100,000, but decided that it wants to reflect the increase in the value of the land in its balance sheet. After professional advice, the current value of the land is determined to be £125,000 – an increase of £25,000.

| Balance sheet | Before revaluation | Revaluation amount | After revaluation |
|---|---|---|---|
| Fixed assets | | | |
| *At cost* | £100,000 | | |
| *At valuation* | | £25,000 | £125,000 |
| Net current assets | £200,000 | | £200,000 |
| Long term liabilities | £50,000 | | £50,000 |
| | £250,000 | £25,000 | £25,000 |
| | | | |
| **Financed by** | | | |
| Share capital | £50,000 | | £50,000 |
| Share premium | £50,000 | | £50,000 |
| Revaluation reserve | | £25,000 | £25,000 |
| Retained reserves | £150,000 | | £150,000 |
| | £50,000 | £25,000 | £75,000 |

Revalued amounts provide the ideal opportunity to boost a balance sheet, with all the benefits that come with greater equity: apparent size, ability to borrow, assets per share, counters to take-overs and so on. What you need to watch are those businesses that revalue upwards rapidly, but aren't in too much of a hurry to revalue downwards. Also look out for smaller businesses for whom there is absolutely no reason whatsoever to show assets at a revalued figure: after all, who are they trying to impress when the shareholders are the same people as the directors? There are plenty of owner-managed businesses whose land is shown at a cost that bears no relation to what a retailing giant might offer them for their prime development site; again, financial statements are not about showing worth in the true sense of the word.

Revaluations provide a complication for depreciation; as you might expect, depreciation should be provided on the revalued amount.

## Depreciation

*Key Management Concept*

Turning now to depreciation, the accounting standard simply says that depreciation must be provided to write off the cost consumed by the business over the asset's useful economic life. So now we have to define cost and life.

Depreciation is set by the business, so there are inevitably differences between identical companies – each can be making the same trading profit, but because of a different view of the world through their depreciation glasses each will be showing a different accounting profit.

Here is a quick example. If we assume that a PC nowadays costs around £900 and has a useful life of three years, then:

|  | 1998 | 1999 | 2000 |
|---|---|---|---|
| Cost of PC | £900 |  |  |
| Net book value at start of year |  | £600 | £300 |
| Annual depreciation charge | £300 | £300 | £300 |
| Net book value at end of year | £600 | £300 | £0 |

For example, take an asset whose cost is £10,000. Assuming a life of 4 years, depreciation would normally be calculated as £2,500 per annum. If we were to assume a residual value at the end of the four year life of £2,000, then the cost 'consumed' by the business over the four years of use now becomes £10,000 less £2,000, or £8,000. Depreciation on £8,000 over 4 years becomes £2,000 per annum.

|  | No residual | Residual |
|---|---|---|
| Original cost of asset | £10,000 | £10,000 |
| Life of asset | 4 years | 4 years |
| Residual value of asset at end of use | £0 | £2,000 |
|  |  |  |
| Annual depreciation | £2,500 | £2,000 |

This all seems eminently sensible, and yet there are some popular misconceptions that seem to abound. Like most fallacies, they have typically grown up by a company seizing upon a genuine concept or principle, and then slowly and quietly distorting its true meaning or definition to suit its own corporate purposes. Depreciation is one such area where such a simple concept (one might think) has developed a Mr Hyde like appearance.

'*Depreciation is there to write the asset down to market value*'. Not true. Look at the example above – there is no way that a second-hand one year old PC whose cost was £900 would be worth £600. In fact, the truth is that accounting statements are most definitely not generally based on the concept of market value, rather on historic cost (or, rarely, revalued amount) less depreciation.

*'Depreciation provides a fund of money for replacement'.* Again, not true. The belief that depreciation is building up a cash pile in the corner of the room is horribly wrong – depreciation is not a cash item and is intangible. In the example above there is not the slightest chance that somewhere there will be £900 of cash at the end of the third year.

The final one that you can *'spend your depreciation'* is simply too terrible to contemplate. Since depreciation is not a cash flow and is purely an internal adjustment, this is way off the mark.

## Depreciation method

Another variable in the depreciation equation is the method of calculation of depreciation; not the life (or rate), but the actual mathematical use to which the life (or rate) is put. There are two main candidates here, although in reality there are many more specialised calculations that can be dusted off and used where appropriate.

Firstly, there is the method that we have already unwittingly seen, called 'straight line on cost'. This method calculates an equal annual amount at the beginning of use of an asset, and maintains the same amount throughout its depreciable life. In the example above (without a residual value) the cost of £10,000 was depreciated in a straight line over the four years. This is so supremely simple as to be actually quite logical. So why do we need the other methods?

The next most commonly used is the 'reducing balance' method. This re-calculates depreciation every year based on the net book value (or written down value) reached to date. Look at the following example of a 25% reducing balance method, and compare it with the 25% straight line on cost method.

|  | Straight line 25% | Reducing balance 25% |
|---|---|---|
| Original cost of asset | £10,000 | £10,000 |
| Depreciation year 1 | 2,500 | 2,500 |
| Net book value end of year 1 | £7,500 | £7,500 |
|  |  |  |
| Net book value b/f | £7,500 | £7,500 |
| Depreciation year 2 | 2,500 | 1,875 |
| Net book value end of year 2 | £5,000 | £5,625 |
|  |  |  |
| Net book value b/f | £5,000 | £5,625 |
| Depreciation year 3 | 2,500 | 1,406 |
| Net book value end of year 3 | £2,500 | £4,219 |
|  |  |  |
| Net book value b/f | £2,500 | £4,219 |
| Depreciation year 4 | 2,500 | 1,055 |
| Net book value end of year 4 | £0 | £3,164 |

One of the interesting properties of the reducing balance method is that you never fully depreciate anything – there will always be a residual amount that is never depreciated, no matter how many years you go forward.

Another of the interesting properties of the reducing balance method is the curvilinear decay of the net book value over time – put simply, it's not a straight line. The diagram below shows how three methods can be plotted over time. Note that it is only the straight line method that decays to nil.

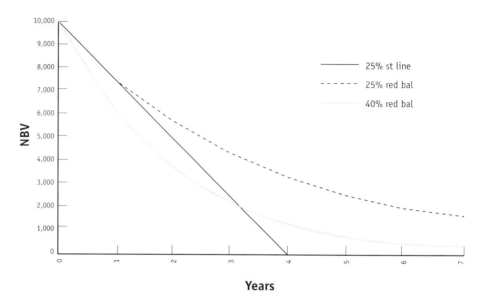

**Years**

So, why bother with the different methods? Looking at the diagram, can you name an everyday asset in a business whose 'worth' might decay in the reducing balance manner? The answer on your lips should be a motor car. Simply driving a new car out of the showroom means you have immediately lost the VAT and the 'newness' premium. What businesses tend to do therefore, so as to get an appropriate 'hit' to the profit and loss account in the early years of ownership, is to choose reducing balance on cars and the like, but at a higher rate (like the 40% above).

Finally, there are just about any number of ways to depreciate assets. Usage remains a firm favourite in certain circles. Take an aeroplane engine, for example, whose life is certified in total flying hours; it obviously makes sense to depreciate it according to the actual number of hours flown. Sometimes the sum-of-digits (an attempt at an 'actuarial' method of allocation) is used, and so on. Whatever is used, remember that it is only the directors trying to adopt a suitable policy so as to write off the cost consumed by the business over the asset's useful economic life.

## Notes to accounts

If you have a set of published accounts, turn to the fixed asset notes. See how the note is laid out in each set of accounts. There are columns for separate classes of asset, adding up to the final total column. There are two main blocks of rows – the first for cost (or valuation), the second for depreciation.

A final row showing block one (cost) less block two (depreciation) – called net book value. It is this year's net book value that is transferred to the face of the balance sheet.

Make sure that you have also inspected closely any note concerning whether land and buildings have been included at a revalued amount rather than cost, the amount and date of the revaluation, and your interpretation of the overall impact: is it realistic? For example, a retail group in 1995 had a note justifying keeping the 1990 valuation of property since 'the group occupied the property for the long-term' and therefore it was not appropriate to show any 'short-term reduction in market value'. An interesting one, that.

Some advanced areas of fixed assets, include the old chestnuts of R&D, capitalised costs, patents, copyright, IPR, goodwill as well as the newer ones such as brands and intangibles. In many of these areas accountants are still all at sea, and have yet to discover the new world of acceptable accounting treatments.

# Current assets and current liabilities

Now let's move on to what is perhaps the most interesting part of the balance sheet: the two sub-headings of Current Assets and Current Liabilities.

Firstly, what does the word Current mean? In the context of Financial Accounts it is very clear, it means within twelve months of the Balance Sheet date. The purpose of current assets is therefore to catch cash now, or anything that will turn into cash within the next twelve months. Whatever does convert into cash within this one year period is very likely to be what is known as an 'operating cycle' or 'trading cycle' item.

We have already seen that businesses can all be divided into two 'cycles', operating and capital investment cycle. The former contains the normal 'buy – do something – sell – collect the cash' transactions, reflecting the daily reality of what the business does, and hence is likely to be measured in days, weeks or a few months at the most (certainly all within a one year period). The latter contains the 'buy fixed assets – renew fixed assets' transactions, reflecting the business need to have fixed assets to enable the business to carry out its trading or operating cycle, and hence is likely to be measured years. The relationship of trading or operating cycle to capital investment cycle will of course depend on the nature of the business and its place along the manufacturing to service spectrum.

## Current assets

If we take as an example a typical manufacturing business and let's say that they make the metal cases for computers. Assuming they already have a factory, equipment and a workforce – what do they need first in order to actually start the operating cycle?

Clearly the answer is to purchase some raw materials as a starting point for the production process. Specifically, in this case, the metal that will be pressed to form the final product.

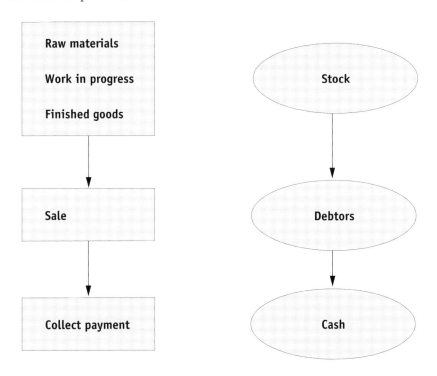

In essence these raw materials will then be turned into finished goods, and somewhere between raw materials and finished goods will lie the category of work in progress.

The raw materials are worked on and become work in progress. This term is beloved by accountants and represents items that are partially completed at the precise moment when the balance sheet photograph is taken. Had the photograph been taken a little while later, the goods may well have been finished. These three items of raw materials, work in progress, and finished

*Best Practice*

goods are collectively known as stock by accountants in financial statements. In reality stock represents nothing more than goods in the operating cycle that will eventually one day convert into cash (and profits!).

If you look at the first item in current assets in a balance sheet you will find stock. The reason for this is that stock is the least liquid of all current assets. In other words it has the furthest to go in order to convert into cash.

We can follow the same process on a bit further. What happens next to these items in stock? The answer is that they are sold (after sitting on a shelf, perhaps) at a profit. Now, sadly, most business transacted is not for cash immediately, so the reality is that a sale gives rise to a debtor – or an amount receivable by the business from its customer.

Finally the customer will pay, and cash is received.

So there we have the three key steps in the operating cycle: stock, debtors and cash. You can see that in any set of accounts these three items are shown, and always in this order. The order is liquidity driven. The least liquid or furthest from conversion into cash (stock) is first, then the next least liquid (debtors) and finally cash itself.

## Working capital example

Let us now try to put a time frame to the two categories of current assets that we have so far encountered. Assuming that the business is pretty slack about stock control, a time of some two months from date of purchase of stock to date of completion of finished goods would not be unreasonable. Ignoring the possibility that stock may simply sit on a shelf for an indeterminate period of time, the next time delay we need to add on reflects simply the fact that customers take at least the credit period offered in order to pay the bills.

For example what do you suppose is an average length of credit by suppliers to their customers? You may very well be surprised to learn that although we remember the number of days as shown on our invoices, that period often bears very little relationship to the actual time taken to pay. Current estimates show that around 48 days is pretty much standard for business conducted within the UK. Interestingly, different countries show markedly different payment period norms, with Greece heading the list at some 240 days and the Germans doing markedly better than our 48 days.

If we are now to add together the 48 days credit period to the two months of stock holding, we now get a total of some three and a half months of cash disadvantage. To put it another way, for every one pound placed in the business' operating cycle, cash is not recovered until nearly four months later. This is referred to as working capital and is the biggest problem financially for almost all commercial businesses.

Comparing our model so far with a typical set of financial statements, you can see that the first two items appearing in current assets are exactly the two things we have seen already. Stock will appear first followed by debtors, and finally cash.

We could be more precise about the downside of having significant amounts of working capital, and to illustrate this let us assume our business makes annual sales of exactly £12 million. With a working capital requirement of approximately four months, we can impute that at any time stock and debtors together could add up to some £4 million in total.

We get this £4 million by taking £12 million annual sales and multiplying by four over twelve.

Of greater concern to the businessman is the impact on profits that this working capital requirement has. If we are to assume a cost of money of some 10%, then we can state that the borrowing cost to maintain a working capital of £4 million would be of the order of some £400,000 per annum. This has a direct impact on a businesses bottom line. If only we could reduce the period from four to three months, we would be adding £100,000 to profits. It sounds too simple, doesn't it?

## Current liabilities

It's not all bad news, however, as we can see when we look at current liabilities. Just as current assets were items that are expected to convert into cash within one year of the balance sheet date, so current liabilities are items that will have to be paid within one year of the balance sheet date.

There are some people in the business world who will lend us money apparently for nothing. These useful people are referred to as creditors. They also play their part in reducing the apparent need for working capital.

Current liabilities typically contain:

- Trade creditors (people owed money because of goods purchased for resale)
- Other creditors (taxation, sundry accruals)
- Bank overdraft (overdrafts are always repayable on demand and hence fall into this category).

You should always see current liabilities in two ways.

Firstly current liabilities record the short-term indebtedness of the enterprise – what will have to be paid out within the next year. With this perspective you don't really want what you owe (current liabilities) to exceed what you have coming in (current assets) – that's a recipe for insolvency. Secondly, however, controlled use of creditors can provide free funding. It's all a question of balance.

## Ratio analysis

*Key Management Concept*

To check the health of the enterprise the current ratio is the traditional measure. Take current assets and divide by current liabilities, and the 'good' answer should be a figure greater than 1. This is just another way of saying that current assets should be more than current liabilities, or that the enterprise has 'positive net current assets'. But to follow the current ratio too slavishly would be to miss the point. For example, if a figure of more than 1 is what text books recommend, then how does this ratio grade an enterprise that is simply too working capital 'fat' (too much stock and debtors). The answer is that it would judge it favourably, yet we all know that wouldn't be correct. So, be aware of following unthinking textbook norms and benchmarks.

Some of the best managed enterprises have negative net current assets. At first sight this might be a recipe for disaster, but a period of quiet reflection will show that all the enterprise is doing is using its creditors as a source of funding. Now, if it is doing this from a position of strength (as the major food retailers do so well) then there is nothing to worry about – unless you happen to be that poor supplier that is being strained. On the other hand, it may be doing it from a position of weakness – it simply can't afford to pay its creditors, and therefore of course you should be worried.

Using our example from before, if we managed to get one month's credit from our suppliers we would reduce the working capital requirement to just three months.

Another example illustrates just how effectively certain business types have successfully managed the complicated balancing act.

You can check these figures for yourself, but my calculations show that the average length of stock-holding in Sainsbury is about 20 days, with the average payment period to suppliers at around 80 days. Which just leaves the credit terms that you are able to negotiate with the checkout assistant as you push your trolley full of shopping. Assuming that you didn't manage to get very far at the checkout, we will accept a figure of zero for debtor days. What this really means is that Sainsbury turn over the stock four times before they need to pay suppliers for the first batch. This is commonly referred to as a cash cow, and is commonplace for most operators who deal predominantly in cash rather than credit. Indeed, some retailers are only still in existence owing to this favourable cash flow characteristic, whereas had they been selling on account their continued well-being may well have been curtailed at a somewhat earlier stage.

The upshot is that what we owe to our suppliers, trade creditors, appears as the first item within current liabilities. This is because, rather like the current asset items, what we owe to our trade creditors will almost certainly have to be paid within one year of the balance sheet date.

## Other current liabilities

So what other types of creditors due within one year are there in a balance sheet? Again, like current assets, the items are ranked in an order of liquidity. This means that trade creditors appear first, and the bank overdraft appears last. Any other items payable within one year will appear in an appropriate order between these two. Typical examples could include sundry business expense accruals, taxation payable on business profits, amounts falling due for payment on hire purchase and leasing commitments and so on.

So what can we make of this? Probably the single most important use is for you, the reader of a set of financial statements, to be able to visualise the business from its current assets and current liabilities – its working capital.

## Critical issues

The point really is that debtors, stock and creditors are often seen as totally unimportant by most managers – simply because they are not part of the traditional profit and loss account. Yet you can easily see how large a potential impact there is to be had upon the profit and loss account simply by controlling elements of working capital better.

# Long-term liabilities

So far then we have looked at fixed assets, current assets and current liabilities. There really is only one item left, and it can be guessed at by looking at the symmetry so far in the balance sheet. If fixed assets are long-term assets, current assets are short-term assets, current liabilities are short-term liabilities, then only long-term liabilities remain.

## Creditors due after more than one year

Long-term liabilities are amounts payable by the business more than one year from the balance sheet date. Typically these items will include long-term bank borrowings, amounts due under hire purchase and leasing agreements more than one year from now, mortgages and formalised borrowing instruments such as debentures and loan stock.

Long-term liabilities can also include things of an accounting technical nature such as provisions, deferrals of income, and deferred taxation. All these things will be looked at briefly in due course.

## Historical cost

We have already seen the accounting convention that states all (well, nearly all) items in a set of UK accounts at historic cost. The value at which these long-term items are shown is normally straightforward, and follows the accounting convention used throughout of 'historical cost'. Unfortunately, some odd items of debt can be disturbingly difficult to pin down (deep discounted bonds, for example). Fortunately these occurrences are few, so the reader can rest assured that what is shown is generally pretty accurate – perhaps it's more a question of what isn't shown that causes the worry.

## Balance sheet summary

That completes the brief review of the balance sheet as prepared under UK principles. All we need to do now is to add it up. The total of assets less liabilities gives the balance sheet total, sometimes referred to as net worth. This is extremely misleading to the uninitiated, who believe that the balance sheet total is therefore an indication as to market value for the business as a whole. Nothing could be further from the truth, and it must always be remembered that the balance sheet total does nothing more than add up the cost less appropriate depreciation of all the assets and liabilities as of the balance sheet date. No mention of market value there, I'm afraid.

# Other side of the balance sheet

*Key Question*

Let's now look at the often misunderstood (and unencountered) 'other' side of the balance sheet. Just as the 'side' that we have been looking at essentially represents the assets less liabilities within the business (where the money is at the time of taking the balance sheet photograph), so the shorter 'side' looks at where the money (or funding) has come from in order to provide those assets.

It stands to reason that the two sides of the balance sheet must show the same figure in total. The constituent parts are essentially two-fold, although there may be several more, all of a technical nature. These two are share capital, and retained reserves.

Share capital is essentially what the shareholders have put into the business, for no guaranteed return. If a company raises, say, £1 million of share capital the Bank Account increases by £1 million as does the Share Capital Account – all nicely in balance! This is the first source of funding.

The second source is the retained reserves, which is essentially the cumulative profits that the enterprise has made since it started out in business. These retained reserves are the most important source (in size) of continued funding for a business. A business that has consistently made profits will have a positive balance on its cumulative reserves, but one which has made cumulative losses will have a deficit on its cumulative reserves – and that deficit has to be 'funded' by someone or something.

# Analysing performance

Chapter 2

# Interpreting accounts using ratio analysis

## Introduction

This section explains the main accounting ratios, tools and techniques used in the interpretation of accounts and financial statements. The most important place to start in the financial analysis of accounts is with the first principles of what we are trying to achieve. It is a common fault that most people preen their profit and loss accounts incessantly, whilst paying only lip service to their balance sheets and cash flow.

As with all the ratios you are about to see, and indeed the ones in common usage within your company, there are quite simply any number of ways to put the figures together. I am constantly surprised at how organisation's own definitions of certain key ratios differs so markedly from the true original, that the use of it in their format is sometimes rather pointless. I also see many companies where there are several different definitions of the same ratio doing the rounds. That certainly makes life difficult for everyone. The point is that it doesn't really matter too much how you calculate ratios, so long as you are consistent in their application and you know what it is that the ratio is telling you.

We therefore need to see how the whole picture fits together, so let's start with the ultimate measure of business performance, return on capital employed.

## Return on capital employed (ROCE)

The numerator (return) is some measure of profit. Normally profit before tax is used, as tax can often be significantly different even between outwardly similar businesses who generate similar profits.

The denominator (capital employed) is some measure of the money tied up in the enterprise.

$$ROCE = \frac{Profit\ before\ tax}{Capital\ employed}$$

Some people approximate capital employed as being the balance sheet total – which is adequate, but not far reaching enough. More accurately capital employed should be shareholders' funds (share capital and reserves – often this is the balance sheet total) plus long-term liabilities. The logic behind adding long-term liabilities is that the lenders of the long-term debt are simply funding the business, in much the same way as the shareholders do, and therefore the better definition of capital employed is to include these items.

Some businesses use the acronym RONA, or return on net assets. If your business is one of these, don't worry, since RONA is the same as ROCE. If we accept capital employed as being shareholders' funds plus long-term liabilities, then all that is left in the balance sheet is fixed assets plus current assets less current liabilities. These items are known as net assets!

Care must be taken when using ROCE as a measure. Both profit and capital employed are subject to variations in definition. In particular, since capital employed is based on the historical cost of assets the return calculated is not a 'real' figure. On the other hand, by comparing the return across industries some meaningful conclusion can be reached. For example heavy manufacturing industries will have low ROCEs, whereas service industries – using less equipment – will have higher returns. Therefore companies in the same industry group should show similar ROCEs and hence variations may indicate lack of efficiency or over-investment in capital assets.

The ROCE is a prime yardstick in assessing a company's profitability. It indicates how successfully a business is utilising its assets. A low return can be because of a low profit margin or a low asset turnover. Conversely a good return is money well invested – indicative of profitability and efficiency.

## Tree of ratios

A business can therefore increase its ROCE by either increasing profits or by decreasing capital employed, or by a combination of the two. This may be rather self-evident, so perhaps what we really need to do now is to analyse how we might take the ratio trail further. To do this we should look at the classic diagram known as the tree of ratios, and this comes in many shapes and sizes. The common thread with any ratio tree, however, is that it simply states the blindingly obvious – that there is the profitability on one side, with asset efficiency on the other. Or, profit and loss compared to balance sheet ratios.

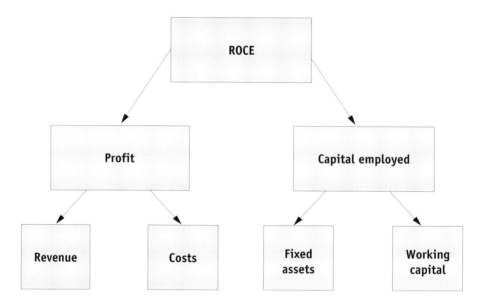

You can see that the left hand branch deals with the profit and loss analysis, whilst the right hand branch examines the balance sheet efficiency. These two critical dimensions of financial statement analysis could not be put more starkly. We all know that we should be looking at both branches of the ratio tree, but how many of us actually do so in our working lives?

# Profitability measures

Taking the profitability measures first, these are likely to be commonly encountered and, frankly, quite well known.

Key Learning Point

### Gross profit margin

$$\text{Gross margin} = \frac{\text{Gross profit}}{\text{Sales}} \times 100\%$$

### Net profit margin

$$\text{Net margin} = \frac{\text{Net profit}}{\text{Sales}} \times 100\%$$

These margins show the profitability of the business. Margins will be constant from period to period unless something changes, costs or sales, relative to each other. Hence a falling profit margin is a sign of increasing costs or declining selling prices – or both.

Classically one would also analyse all the costs involved in the business, expressing each cost as a percentage of sales so that they can all be added down in the same manner.

### Costs as percentage of sales

$$\text{Cost} = \frac{\text{Cost}}{\text{Sales}} \times 100\%$$

Often these results are informative as to whether costs are behaving as fixed or variable costs, and whether the trend is one of improvement or worsening.

## Earnings per share (EPS)

*Key Management Concept*

Of lesser importance for unquoted companies, this is a very important ratio which must be disclosed at the bottom of the profit and loss account for listed companies.

$$EPS = \frac{\text{Profit after tax}}{\text{Number of ordinary shares}}$$

As will be discussed later, the EPS is used by investors in calculating the price earnings ratio (or P/E) ratio. This is simply defined as follows:

$$P/E \text{ ratio} = \frac{\text{Market price of share}}{\text{Earnings per share}}$$

The P/E ratio expresses the number of years' earnings represented by the current market price and is the major indicator of the market's view of the company. The significance of the P/E ratio can only be judged in relation to the ratios of other companies in the same kind of business, although as a general rule a higher P/E ratio – share price racing ahead of earnings – shows that the market is confident of the company's prospects.

# Balance sheet measures

Turning now to the balance sheet measures, these are likely to be less commonly encountered and, frankly, almost unknown to most people.

## Asset turnover

This indicates how well a company is utilising its assets and is calculated as follows:

$$\text{Asset turnover} = \frac{\text{Sales}}{\text{Capital employed}}$$

This ratio is similar to ROCE except that it deals with sales generated by the assets rather than profits generated by the assets. A low asset turnover can indicate over-investment in capital assets or that the company is not generating a sufficient volume of business for its size. Again, the type of industry involved will play a large part and, as with ROCE, service industries should show higher values than manufacturing industries.

However it suffers from the same problems as ROCE with the book values of capital employed, since revaluing the assets of a company would automatically reduce this ratio without the business having changed at all. As we have seen capital employed most usually comprises share and loan capital together with any profits already retained in the business.

## Fixed asset turnover

As a sub-division, you can calculate fixed asset turnover: replacing total assets by fixed assets.

*Key Learning Point*

## Debtor days

This is computed by dividing the year end trade debtors figure by the average daily sales. Average daily sales (sales per day) is arrived at by dividing total annual sales by 365.

$$\text{Sales per day} = \frac{\text{Total annual sales}}{365}$$

$$\text{Average collection period} = \frac{\text{Debtors}}{\text{Sales per day}}$$

This ratio is also known as 'days sales in debtors'. If a company has a standard payment term of 30 days on its sales then its average collection period should be close to 30 days. This would indicate that debts are being paid on time and that there is a steady stream of cash coming in. However if the days sales in debtors increases then this indicates that customers are taking longer to pay. Once debts get very old they are harder to collect, so a high average collection period could indicate that debtors may include amounts that will not be paid. It could also suggest that the company has customers who are unwilling to pay for some reason, perhaps unsatisfactory service.

However there are very good reasons why a firm has a high average collection period. Overseas customers and public sector bodies are notoriously slow payers although the cash is usually received in the end. Often companies do sometimes give extended credit terms to major clients. Therefore other information about the type of business is necessary before an informed judgement can be made.

## Stock days

$$\text{Stock days} = \frac{\text{Stock} \times 365}{\text{Cost of sales}}$$

This ratio is probably more used than stock turnover, (which is the reciprocal of stock days) although ultimately it measures the same thing. Notice how this ratio is similar to the debtor days calculation earlier, the key difference being in the fraction's denominator. Whereas for debtor days we divide by sales (since making a sale is what gives rise to the debtor), here we divide stock by cost of sales (since that is where the stock will end up being shown in the profit and loss account).

## Creditor days

$$\text{Creditor days} = \frac{\text{Creditors} \times 365}{\text{Cost of sales}}$$

This ratio is similar in outlook to debtor days, in as much as it measures the efficiency (or speed) of payment of a company's suppliers. High creditor days can mean extremely efficient purchasing techniques on the one hand, and it can simply be that there is insufficient money to pay the suppliers.

## Current ratio

$$\text{Current ratio} = \frac{\text{Current assets}}{\text{Current liabilities}}$$

This is a common method of analysing working capital (net current assets) and is generally accepted as the measure of short-term solvency of a company. It indicates the extent to which the claims of short-term creditors are covered by the assets that are expected to be converted to cash in a period roughly corresponding to the maturity of the claims.

Where a company is showing falling current ratios then its liquidity may be a problem. In the extreme situation where current assets are less than current liabilities, were the current creditors to call in their debts, then the company would have to sell some of their fixed assets to meet their creditors' demands.

However, care has to be taken when considering this figure. Current assets comprise stocks, debtors and cash; therefore when a company is in a market where large stocks must be held to meet immediate customer demand or where industry standard credit terms are longer than average, that company will have high current assets and hence a high current ratio.

On the other hand, where stocks and debtors are relatively small due to the sales being mainly cash and stock levels being kept as low as possible, current assets will be small and hence the current ratio will look low. Therefore, once again, comparisons must be made across an industry or over several periods to see if a general trend emerges which might give the true picture.

## Quick ratio

*Key Learning Point*

The quick (or liquidity) ratio is based on the assumption that stocks will not be recovered quickly enough to meet the time scale for the payment of creditors, and the business must therefore look to its debtors and cash balances to cover the current liabilities. The quick ratio, sometimes referred to as the 'acid test', is therefore calculated as follows:

$$\text{Quick ratio} = \frac{\text{Current assets less stock}}{\text{Current liabilities}}$$

As with the current ratio the quick ratio must be compared across an industry if it is to be a meaningful measurement. The traditional thinking was that this ratio should not be less than 1, but bearing in mind the differences in levels of debtors and the nature of outstanding liabilities there should be no general rule. Many companies operate successfully with quick ratios of less than 1, since the ratio only becomes a problem if the creditors call in the amounts due to them unexpectedly. Clever cash flow management can eliminate the problems of such a deficit. Again there will be a norm for a particular business or type of business.

## Stock to net assets

$$\text{Stock to net current assets} = \frac{\text{Stock x 100\%}}{\text{Net current assets}}$$

This ratio indicates the importance of stock as a percentage of working capital. The following conclusions could be drawn from too high a percentage:

a) stocks are too high in relation to the financial resources of the business

b) poor stock control exists

c) obsolete stocks are being held.

On the other hand some businesses may require high levels of stock to be held if customers expect delivery on demand or if many different lines need to be kept. It is therefore important to compare companies in the same line of business who face the same demands on their stock and debtors.

## Stock turnover

$$\text{Stock turnover} = \frac{\text{Cost of sales}}{\text{Stock}}$$

This ratio is useful in indicating the rate of movement of stock.

This can vary tremendously between types of business. A local baker, for example, sells all its stock every day. Therefore the average stock will be low in comparison to cost of sales for the year. On the other hand a boat builder may only build five boats each year, so at a given time his stock will be much higher as a proportion of cost of goods sold in that year.

A high stock turnover, within an industry, is generally regarded as a sign of efficiency. However in some cases it can mean that a firm is living 'from hand to mouth'.

# Finance ratios

*Key Management Concept*

## Gearing/borrowing ratio

This measures the proportion of capital employed that has been raised by fixed interest loans (and preference share capital) as opposed to equity capital.

$$\text{Gearing ratio} = \frac{\text{Debt finance (short and long term loans)}}{\text{Total capital employed (debt and equity)}}$$

Creditors will often prefer lower gearing ratios since the more debt finance a company has the higher its interest commitments will be and the less cash it will have to pay its creditors. But there are some tax advantages to debt finance, as well as a greater overall flexibility.

Gearing also varies tremendously between types of company, with some companies having more debt than equity and others having no long-term debt at all. It is one of the most complicated areas of analysis and has been the topic of much financial discussion and theory.

What you are really trying to get an answer to is the questions 'Why have they borrowed money, and what have they done with it? Is it to sensibly expand and grow the business, or is it to plug holes in the cash flow?' One is a valid reason, whilst the other you might look at less favourably.

## Interest cover

This measures the comfort level of interest payments made annually.

$$\text{Interest cover} = \frac{\text{Profit before interest and tax}}{\text{Interest payable}}$$

For example, we as individuals all have the concept of interest cover – how many times could you afford to pay your mortgage out of your net monthly salary? If you are at the beginning of your career, the answer may well be between 1 and 2 (hopefully it will be more than 1). At the end of you career, the mortgage bill may simply be less onerous – so your interest cover may be in double digits.

Exactly the same principles apply to businesses and the interest they pay. As you might guess, when the economic cycle downturns then interest rates rise just at the same time as profits go walkabout.

# Match the business with ratios

*Activity*

On the following pages is an example that gets you to think about ratios, their uses and their limitations a little more closely.

Your task is to match the five businesses listed below with the columns of precalculated ratios. You should make reference to the list of proforma ratios on the pages that follow. For a moderate degree of difficulty, you should be able to get the correct answers just by using ratios 1 to 5 inclusive. You can see that ratio 1 is the overall king ratio – ROCE. Ratios 2 and 3 are measures of profitability, whilst ratios 4 and 5 address the balance sheet.

The five businesses are:

1. An electrical engineering manufacturer.

2. A large chain of shops retailing household white goods.

3. A package holiday company providing inclusive holidays in the UK and overseas.

4. A chain of betting shops.

5. A fresh food manufacturer producing 'own label' high quality foods.

Your task is to say which column of ratios (A, B, C, D or E) belongs to which business. On the following page is an explanation of the calculation of the ratios.

|  | Ratio | A | B | C | D | E |
|---|---|---|---|---|---|---|
| 1 | ROCE | 68% | 17% | 21% | 28% | 3% |
| 2 | Gross profit | 57% | 12% | 13% | 24% | 18% |
| 3 | Net profit | 32% | 4% | 7% | 7% | 0% |
| 4 | Debtors' age (days) | 0 | 88 | 0 | 44 | 4 |
| 5 | Age of stock (days) | 5 | 108 | 81 | 22 | 0 |
| 6 | Asset turnover | 5.2 | 5.1 | 2.9 | 3.7 | 8.6 |
| 7 | Financial leverage | 1.12 | 1.06 | 1.1 | 1.09 | 1.1 |
| 8 | Interest cover | n/a | 11 | 4 | 38 | n/a |
| 9 | Current ratio | 0.22 | 1.01 | 1.48 | 1.20 | 1.15 |
| 10 | Quick ratio | 0.20 | 0.49 | 0.80 | 0.89 | 1.15 |
| 11 | Fixed asset turnover | 3.1 | 5.0 | 4.1 | 3.8 | 13.1 |

# Proforma ratios

| 1 | ROCE | = | $\dfrac{\text{Profit before tax}}{\text{Shareholders funds}}$ |
|---|---|---|---|
| 2 | Gross margin | = | $\dfrac{\text{Gross profit}}{\text{Sales}}$ |
| 3 | Net profit | = | $\dfrac{\text{Net profit before tax}}{\text{Sales}}$ |
| 4 | Debtors age | = | $\dfrac{365 \times \text{closing trade debtors}}{\text{Credit sales}}$ |
| 5 | Age of stock | = | $\dfrac{365 \times \text{closing stock}}{\text{Cost of goods sold}}$ |
| 6 | Asset turnover | = | $\dfrac{\text{Sales}}{\text{Net assets}}$ |
| 7 | Financial leverage | = | $\dfrac{\text{Assets} - \text{short-term liabilities}}{\text{Shareholders funds}}$ |
| 8 | Interest cover | = | $\dfrac{\text{Profit before interest}}{\text{Interest payable}}$ |
| 9 | Current ratio | = | $\dfrac{\text{Current assets}}{\text{Current liabilities}}$ |
| 10 | Quick ratio | = | $\dfrac{\text{Current assets} - \text{stock}}{\text{Current liabilities}}$ |
| 11 | Fixed asset turnover | = | $\dfrac{\text{Sales}}{\text{Fixed assets}}$ |

# Match the business with ratios: *solution*

The five businesses are as follows:

A   is company 4, a chain of betting shops.

B   is company 1, an electrical engineering manufacturer.

C   is company 2, a large chain of shops retailing household white goods.

D   is company 5, a fresh food manufacturer producing 'own label' high quality foods.

E   is company 3, a package holiday company providing inclusive holidays in the UK and overseas.

The logic of the answers runs something like this. Ironically you may well find that the more and harder that you think about the problems, the less easy it is to get the correct answer.

I always find that it is easier to 'visualise' the days in working capital rather than anything else. For example, A and E are similar in that they are both cash businesses (no debtors) and service businesses (no stocks). The only two options that really fit these descriptions are companies 3 and 4. Since we cannot tell the difference any further than just using the working capital ratios, we now have to turn to the profitability measures. These show straight away that A is hugely profitable, whilst E is not. Clearly A has to be company 4, therefore E has to be company 3.

You can get the next step right by asking the simple question 'Would I rather eat a 108, 81 or 22 day old yoghurt'? The answer must be none of the above, but since one has to be correct you could guess that D is in fact company 5.

A quick inspection of B suggests a manufacturer high stock and debtor days, B must therefore be company 1. That leaves C as company 2, which just about fits the profitability margins and the working capital days.

All in all not too difficult, provided you think (and guess, quite often) as to what you would imagine the business to look like. In our next example we will be getting more technical with the calculations, but in the meantime the next few pages look at practical ways in which you can influence your working capital.

## Practical working capital management

*Key Management Concept*

This section explains the basic principles and techniques used in working capital management. It is really no more than a statement of the obvious best practice techniques for any organisation.

### Debtors

*Action Checklist*

- Reduce time from placement of order by customer to receipt of goods

- Reduce time taken to invoice customers

- Reduce debt collection period

- Bank receipts on a daily basis

- Avoid part deliveries, or other situations which give customers an excuse to delay payment

- Issue statements of account promptly

- Avoid despatching large quantities of orders late in the month; despatches made in the last few days of the month may not be received by the customer until the following month, thereby delaying payment by the customer

- Consider paying salesmen commission based on speed of collection of debtors and not on sales value

- Maintain personal contact with customers

- Prompt payment discounts

- Payment in advance from slow/high risk payers

- Factor debts.

## Stock

- Establish stock reporting systems to provide stock turnover, ageing analysis, obsolescence and monitor trends

- Consider reducing storage capacity – excess capacity tempts overstocking

- Review supplier lead time and reduce stockholdings accordingly

- Monitor old, surplus and obsolete stock

- Ensure an appropriate balance of stock is held between raw materials, work-in-progress and finished goods

- Critical path analysis performed on production times will highlight points of high and low stock requirements

- Bulk-buying may not be worth the discounts received if not quickly converted into cash

- Order economic quantities

- Refuse early deliveries if costly in terms of stock holding costs

- Co-ordinate sales and production forecasts

- Consider investment in more efficient machinery to reduce work-in-progress and increase throughput

- Consider reducing production batch sizes

- Despatch finished goods promptly

- Review distribution network and stock – holding locations; increased transportation costs incurred by centralising warehousing may be less than storage at several locations

- Do not hold excessive stocks of poor profit earners, leaving insufficient space for high margin lines

- Handle returns quickly.

## Creditors

*Action Checklist*

- Negotiate extended terms with suppliers

- Payment on predetermined dates will maintain good supplier relationships

- Maintain contact with suppliers

- In times of cash flow problems, payment of small amounts first may ensure continuation of regular supply

- Payment by cheque rather than by bank transfer generates slight cash flow advantage.

# Detailed case study

Overleaf is the profit and loss accounts and balance sheets for an industrial supply wholesaler. It is a real life businesses, only the name has been changed. You have financial information for three consecutive years.

## Analysis

Using the techniques learnt so far, analyse the performance of the companies:

- Is it profitable?

- Has it the potential to lose control over their liquidity?

- Is it a company that you would do business with?

## Helpful hints

Start with the profit and loss account for the time being.

What do you normally do when you are faced with a set of figures like this? Some people are what I call 'Year on year' analysts. They say 'Sales are up (which they are), but so is cost of sales' and so on. What this approach misses is any feeling of exactly whether things are really in line.

What you need to do therefore, as a first step, is to 'common size' the profit and loss account. That is to say, express each cost as a percentage of sales, right the way down to the bottom line. This then gives you the solid basis on which to make assessments about whether things have moved in line with expectations, or whether things are getting out of hand.

### RICHARD LIMITED

*Profit and Loss Accounts*

|  | 1997 | 1996 | 1995 |
|---|---|---|---|
| Turnover | 3,600 | 3,000 | 2,000 |
| Cost of Sales | 2,900 | 2,400 | 1,600 |
| **Gross profit** | 700 | 600 | 400 |
| Distribution costs | 162 | 135 | 91 |
| Administrative expenses | 360 | 235 | 175 |
| **Operating profit** | 178 | 230 | 134 |
| Interest payable | 32 | 15 | 21 |
| **Profit before taxation** | 146 | 215 | 113 |
| Taxation payable | 35 | 52 | 27 |
| **Profit for the year** | 111 | 163 | 86 |
| Dividends | 40 | 33 | 0 |
| **Retained profit for the year** | 71 | 130 | 86 |

## RICHARD LIMITED

### *Balance Sheets*

|  | 1997 | 1996 | 1995 |
|---|---|---|---|
|  | £ | £ | £ |
| **Fixed Assets** | | | |
| Tangible assets | 197 | 55 | 51 |
| **Current Assets** | | | |
| Stocks | 654 | 553 | 363 |
| Debtors | 741 | 596 | 421 |
| Cash in hand | 31 | 33 | 23 |
| *Total* | 1,426 | 1,182 | 807 |
| **Creditors due within one year** | | | |
| Trade and other creditors | 401 | 407 | 332 |
| Taxation | 35 | 52 | 27 |
| Finance leases | 55 | 19 | 18 |
| Bank overdraft | 737 | 437 | 282 |
| *Total* | 1,228 | 915 | 659 |
| *Net Current Assets* | 198 | 267 | 148 |
| **Creditors due after one year** | 32 | 30 | 37 |
| *Net worth* | 363 | 292 | 162 |
| | | | |
| **Capital and Reserves** | | | |
| Called-up share capital | 25 | 25 | 25 |
| Profit and loss account | 338 | 267 | 137 |
| *Total* | 363 | 292 | 162 |

Have a first attempt before turning the page over and looking at the answers.

## Profit and loss account analysis

The first thing to do is to look at the individual lines within the profit and loss account for each year. By expressing everything as a percentage of sales in that year you will be developing a yardstick that you can use to compare between years. Here is the profit and loss account after 'common-sizing'.

### RICHARD LIMITED

*Profit and Loss Accounts*

|  | 1997 | % sls | 1996 | % sls | 1995 | % sls |
|---|---|---|---|---|---|---|
| **Turnover** | 3,600 | 100% | 3,000 | 100% | 2,000 | 100% |
| Cost of Sales | 2,900 | 81% | 2,400 | 80% | 1,600 | 80% |
| **Gross profit** | 700 | 19% | 600 | 20% | 400 | 20% |
| Distribution costs | 162 | 5% | 135 | 5% | 91 | 5% |
| Administrative expenses | 360 | 10% | 235 | 8% | 175 | 9% |
| **Operating profit** | 178 | 5% | 230 | 8% | 134 | 7% |
| Interest payable | 32 | 1% | 15 | 1% | 21 | 1% |
| **Profit before taxation** | 146 | 4% | 215 | 7% | 113 | 6% |
| Taxation payable | 35 | 1% | 52 | 2% | 27 | 1% |
| **Profit for the year** | 111 | 3% | 163 | 5% | 86 | 4% |
| Dividends | 40 | 1% | 33 | 1% | 0 | 0% |
| **Retained profit for the year** | 71 | 2% | 130 | 4% | 86 | 4% |

*sls = sales*

So what can we tell from this?

We can see that the gross margin is similar year to year – 20%, 20% and 19%. Now a 1% drop in gross is not likely to be to worrying, but it is worth pointing out that 1% of the sales in 1997 of £3.6m is worth around £36,000 – or 50% of the retained profits for the year!

The sales figure looks good however – good growth from year to year, and sales are booming.

Looking down at the operating profit line we can see that whilst things improved in 1996, they worsened in 1997. The operating margin improvement to 8% in 1996 (from 7% in 1995) was eradicated in 1997, as operating profit slumped to a meagre 5%. What has caused this, given that the gross margin has more or less stood up?

The answer lies in either distribution or administration costs. Distribution is a steady 5% each year: the hallmark of a true variable cost. Administration, on the other hand, has risen in 1997 to 10% of sales, a worsening of two percentage points on the reported 8% of sales in 1996. This 2% and the disappearance of 1% of gross margin accounts for the drop in operating profit from 7% to 4%.

Reading on down, interest payable is increasing in £s (increased interest rates and/or increased amount borrowed), and it looks as though the directors have started to pay dividends (avoiding national insurance on salary).

You can almost feel what is going on in the mind of the board: business and sales are booming, so let's take some reward for it all. The consequence is that while sales are going up, the level of retained profits is not going up proportionately.

## Balance sheet analysis

Turning to the balance sheet, just run your eyes down the figures, calculating where necessary. The first thing that hits you should be the increased level of fixed assets. It looks as though they have bought a significant amount of fixed assets. Here you hope that the assets are productive plant and equipment, rather than a new BMW or a head office.

In a more scientific vein, calculate the working capital – namely stock, debtor and creditor days. You should come up with figures that look like these.

| | | | | | | |
|---|---|---|---|---|---|---|
| Stock days | | 82 days | | 84 days | | 83 days |
| Debtor days | | 75 days | | 73 days | | 77 days |
| Creditor days | | 50 days | | 62 days | | 76 days |
| | *Sub-total* | 107 days | | 95 days | | 84 days |

What this shows is a pretty consistent picture on the stock and debtor days – although consistently longer than you might think. What is really playing havoc with the working capital is the fact that he is paying his trade creditors more quickly. Cynically, this only happens for one of two reasons. Either he is paying them sooner because he is taking advantage of an early settlement discount, or he is being squeezed to simply pay sooner. We could easily discount the first theory, since the gross margin worsening does not indicate that lower cost of sales have been negotiated.

We can also see quite clearly that the bank overdraft has simply got out of hand. Perhaps because of this there is greater reliance on leasing at the end of the year. Things do not look good, and we have been able to tell all of this by some very simple analysis.

It is important to stress here that whilst the profit and loss account may not have looked too bad, the balance sheet is not very encouraging. Bearing in mind the fact that we tend to be blind to the balance sheet, and focus on the profit and loss to excess, we might not have spotted that this business is in real trouble.

It is in fact guilty of overtrading, a condition where the following three things happen:

- Low gross margin.

- High working capital.

- Growth.

We will examine the exact relationship later, but for the moment we will use this example to build up the third financial statement (the one we have not yet seen): the Cash Flow Statement (FRS1).

The best way to see an FRS1 cash flow statement is to work through one. What you see overleaf is the FRS1 for this business already calculated.

**RICHARD LIMITED**

*Cash Flow Analysis*

| | | |
|---|---:|---:|
| **Operating profit** | 178 | |
| Increase in stocks | (101) | |
| Increase in debtors | (145) | |
| Decrease in creditors | (6) | |
| | | (74) |
| **Returns on inv. & ser of finance** | | |
| Interest payable | (32) | |
| Dividends paid | (40) | |
| | | (72) |
| **Taxation** | | |
| Corporation tax paid | | (52) |
| **Investing activities** | | |
| Purchase of fixed assets | | (142) |
| Cash flow before financing | | (340) |
| **Financing** | | |
| Increase in overdraft | 300 | |
| Increase in long term creditors | 2 | |
| Increase in finance leases | 36 | |
| | | 338 |
| *Cash flow after financing* | | (2) |
| Opening cash balance | 33 | |
| Closing cash balance | 31 | |
| *Movement in cash balances* | | (2) |

Make sure that you have got one finger in the profit and loss account and balance sheet, and begin to tick up the cash flow statement above. First, find where the £178 in the first line comes from. The answer is the operating profit in the profit and loss account. Do not forget that this is the profit as measured on the accruals basis, and yet what we want is to turn it into cash from profits – in other words we want to strip out the accruals. We do this by adjusting for the next three lines, the first of which is called Increase in stocks.

Where has this figure come from? You should be able to calculate it from the difference between the 1996 and 1997 balance sheet stock figures. Stock has simply gone up by £101 from 1996 to 1997, and this of course must mean that there is more of the business's money tied up in a larger stock pile.

Working capital can often be thought of as a sponge – if you leave it uncontrolled it will suck up any spare cash into stock and debtors. To control working capital you need to squeeze the sponge, and you will get cash in exchange for lower stock and debtors.

Sadly, in this instance, the increase in stock means a use of cash, which is why the figure of £101 has brackets around it.

What about the next figure – the increase in debtors? Well, exactly the same logic applies here, in as much as larger debtors of £145 must mean less cash in the bank account. So another bracketed figure appears, and we have already trashed our profit figure of £178. This business is cash negative at the operating level. It needs money shovelling into it to feed the working capital monster every time sales increase.

But we haven't finished yet, as he has even got his creditors going the wrong way. Normally in an expanding business you might expect to lean on your suppliers a bit more, but in this case the reverse has happened. Another cash negative hits the cash flow statement.

The subtotal of £74 is the cash generated from operations, and is the most important figure in the cash flow statement. This business, whilst growing, will never pay its way in cash terms. That puts the dividend and purchase of fixed assets into a slightly different light now, doesn't it? Perhaps they weren't such clever moves, after all.

Completing the cash flow statement, the next section with interest and dividends is quite simple, albeit another net cash drain.

The taxation figure paid in 1997 is actually 1996's liability: tax is paid nine months after the company's accounting year end.

The fixed asset addition of £142 is simply the difference between the fixed asset figures in the balance sheet.

All of the above items add up to give a total cash bleed of £340 for the year in question – quite a different feel from the acceptable profit and loss account we saw earlier. So how has he managed to keep the ship afloat?

There are three sources of funding that have been taken advantage of. The most significant is the bank overdraft, which has increased by some £300. There are short and long-term creditors (lease and hire purchase liabilities) which have increased by £2 and £36. These sources give a total of £338, which very nearly goes to offset the cash bleed of £340 – but not quite.

The final point of a cash flow statement is that the net cash worsening of £2 should be the difference between the cash figure at 1996 compared to 1997 – and it is! The joy of a cash flow statement is that everything adds up and is provable.

Now, although most people say 'Yes' when asked if they know the difference between cash and profits, actually doing a cash flow statement is extremely instructive. This business had the plug pulled on it by the bank, which is hardly surprising since the directors were clearly not in control of it. That might seem a little harsh to those profit and loss maniacs out there who see rising sales, market share and so on – but who cannot see the impact of it all on the balance sheet.

## A calculation

Here is possibly one of the most useful calculations that you will come across. It generally works in most businesses, but be aware that its overall accuracy is only as good as the underlying accounts themselves.

Just calculate each item of working capital – stock, debtors and creditors, as a percentage of sales. You will get something like this:

| | | |
|---|---|---|
| Stock as % sales | 18.2% | £654 |
| Debtors as % sales | 20.6% | £741 |
| Creditors as % sales | (11.1%) | (£401) |
| *Net working assets* | 27.6% | £994 |

This figure of net working assets is simply the amount of extra working capital needed for every extra pound of sales – in this case the figure is 28p for every extra pound of sales.

The theory then goes on to say that whilst we need 28p extra for every £1 of sales, we actually get something towards that from the gross margin. In this year the gross margin was 19%, which is not enough to keep the fires stoked (we need 28%). The result is that this business is cash negative to the tune of 9p in the £1 (28% less 19% = 9%), which partially explains the poor cash performance this year.

To turn the business into a cash cow, however, need not be all that difficult: reduce stock a little, reduce debtors a little, lean on suppliers a little and increase the gross margin a little! Simple, really!

This little calculation is a sort of quick alternative to a cash flow statement, and one of its great uses is that it can be used proactively. You can estimate, for example, the additional funding needed if incremental business were to be taken on.

## Break-even

Although break-even is covered later in this book, before you move on from this example it might be useful to calculate a break-even point and see how it is moving.

A break-even is simply the fixed costs divided by the gross margin. For this example (as we do generally when just presented with a set of financial accounts) we assume the distribution and administration costs to be fixed.

With fixed costs of £522 (£162 plus £360), we now divide by the gross margin of 19%. This gives a break-even sales point of £2,685. Since sales are running at £3,600 we are clearly making a profit. We normally express our comfort with the situation as calculated by the 'margin of safety'. This is the amount we are actually trading at, expressed as a percentage over the break-even.

In 1997 we would be trading at £915 (£3,600 over £2,685) above the break-even of £2,685. This is equal to a margin of safety of 34% over break-even sales. This is worrying, since in the previous year we had been trading at a margin of safety of 62%.

# External analysis

Chapter 3

# A source of intelligence

The second section in the Financial Times is where all the financial action is, and there is obviously a lot more than we can cover here. All I really want to do is to make sure that you fully understand a few key measures, and can work your way around the information.

## News stories

Assuming that you have found your way through the opening pages in section two, with the aid of the contents, you will quickly discover that the company news gets more foreign and eventually leads into the commodity prices, foreign exchange and other items.

## Back page

It is now time to turn to the outside back page of section two, and study the copious amounts of information given there.

The top few rows is called the Market Report (for London, in the UK version of the *Financial Times*), and obviously discusses the major influences and outcomes in the London Stock Exchange for the day.

The next block is titled 'Main Movers' and lists those companies with remarkable share price movements. Clearly any business 'in the news' will have a write-up here. Read carefully, as some of the underlying reasons behind the movements may appear paper-thin to the uninitiated outsider.

Much of the rest is devoted to detail, but for the want of looking you could arm yourself with very interesting facts. Take for example the two feint lines beneath the section on 'Hourly Movements'. Here you can find not only the time of the day's high and low, but also the rather more important year's high and low of the FTSE overall. This is very important in determining how your chosen share has moved relative to the index as a whole.

## Major quoted companies

The FTSE index everyone tends to refers to is the FTSE 100 (Financial Times Stock Exchange). The 100 takes as its constituents the largest 100 UK quoted companies, as measured by their overall worth – known as market capitalisation. Every so often there is a highly significant promotion/relegation battle that goes on to decide the top 100. Recently there have been additions in the form of the recently floated former building societies, rather like some years ago we had the privatised utilities such as water and electricity. Actually, some commentators suggest that not all of these recently privatised companies are real commercial businesses at all, and that their presence in the FTSE 100 is a distraction!

## FTSE 100

Being in the top FTSE 100 is critical for a business as you instantly go on everyone's buy list, which immediately has the rather nice effect of boosting your share price – and vice versa, of course.

At this point many people quite rightly ask two questions. Firstly, what difference does its share price make to a company? Secondly, what is this thing called the FTSE, what units is it measured in, and who sets it?

## Share prices

Share prices are totally irrelevant for companies on one level. Of course the actual price at which shares are traded will in no way affect the daily production or selling routines within a business. However, the market's perceived worth of a company may well affect its own ability to borrow or raise more funds from the investment community. After all, if it hasn't exactly done well with the last lot of money, why should it be lent some more? Ultimately, if the value falls far enough then there will be certain attractions for the vultures. Rather like a car scrapyard can make more money by selling the parts from an old car piecemeal, so an asset stripper may find a poorly performing company attractive for the same reasons. We must not forget the final point that since much of a senior executive's pay will be through share options, then there will be an inevitable concern for the share price.

## FTSE movements

The second point about the FTSE is a surprisingly common complaint. The index is just that – it plots the relative movement in the basket of 100 shares. In early 1998 the index reached 6,100, whereas just a year previously it stood at 4,000. This 50% increase has not, however, been the norm. It is fascinating to look at the movements in the light of world events, political party governing the UK, interest rates and inflation. At the time of the Gulf War in 1991 the index momentarily dipped below 2,000, whilst in the Thatcher 1980s it was still grappling with the 1,000 mark. All the index really tries to do is to show the relative movements in the worth of the basket of 100 shares – so in fact there is no magical hand that sets the index! The other point to be aware of is that the index is weighted, so that movements in the share price of a larger constituent company will move the index more than a similar share price movement in a smaller constituent company.

## Share data

So, turn back one page from the outside back page, and look at the UK FTSE companies in their full glory. Note how the shares are grouped into quite distinct sections, something which is terribly important to all concerned since it is relative performance within a sector that is closely observed.

Whilst there are many things of interest on these pages, and indeed there is a very helpful 'Financial Times Guide' on the bottom right hand side of the right hand page, we will focus on just the key elements. Taking a sample share you should be able to easily spot its price (mid market, previous day's closing price), change on the day (from previous day's close), range of price (previous 52 weeks moving window period), and then some other columns! Depending on the day of the week, these other columns could be market capitalisation, trading volume, yield gross or price earnings.

## Market capitalisation

This is calculated by multiplying the number of shares that the company has issued (a finite and known figure) by the share price (a fluctuating figure). Market capitalisation therefore gives a crude estimate of a company's worth in the marketplace, except of course that any real bid to take over a company would result in the share price increasing (you would hope). In early 1998 a market capitalisation of around £3 billion gets you into the FTSE 100.

Trading volume really defines itself, and is somewhat interesting to help you keep track of the popularity of your shares, and provide an indication of significant activity levels.

Of the last two indicators – yield gross and price earnings – the latter is the more important. In order to understand price earnings we need to look at something called earnings per share (EPS).

## Price earnings – computation

EPS is the pivotal measure that, many analysts say, encompasses all you need to know about corporate performance. To calculate it all you do is divide the profit after tax made by a company by the number of shares in issue. The result is the profit that each share has generated, according to the latest set of financial statements, or EPS. This benchmark is then compared with previous years EPS, and the expectation is that future EPS will continue to grow. As you will no doubt appreciate the profit that each share generates may not be the amount by which you, the shareholder, benefits. Instead that is measured by the dividend (or dividend per share) – discussed later.

So, apart from charting a hopefully upward trend in EPS, what else is it used for? You could probably work this out for yourself, but if you expressed the current share price as a multiple of the profit that a share made last year, then you might have a useful relative measure. What you have just calculated is the P/E ratio, or the multiple – the numbers of times a share is currently valued at compared to the profits that the share made last year. We do exactly this sort of thing when we express house prices as a multiple of average earnings, to get a feel for whether houses are currently cheap or expensive.

*Key Learning Point*

## Price earnings – comparison

EPS and the P/E ratio are taken very seriously by the market. Companies in the same line of business should have similar ratios. If the average P/E ratio for a group of companies in the same industry is 8 then a ratio of 14 for one particular company suggests that the shares of that company are in great demand, probably because a rapid growth of earnings is expected. A low ratio, say 3 for example, indicates that a company is not favoured by investors and probably has poor future prospects.

Thus the P/E ratio is a good indication as to how the market views the prospects of a firm, and a constantly falling value can indicate a company in which investors are losing confidence.

The whole point of computing the P/E is so that we can then compare between companies. For example, if you look at the 'Retailers Food' section in the Financial Times it is pretty obvious which companies are strong in the sector – Sainsbury, Tesco and latterly ASDA (high teens and twenties). All of their P/E ratios are likely to be well ahead of the stragglers. Put simply, a board of directors wake up in the morning and ask why their P/E is so low compared to the competition, and just what is it they can do about it? The answer is that they can massage the top line in the fraction (share price) or the bottom line (earnings per share). When you actually begin to think about cause and effect, however, the picture gets a little muddied. For example, is it just the ever-increasing level of profits that will push the P/E ratio to even dizzier heights, or is it in some way linked to more than that – quality of business, product, management and so on?

There are caveats to using the P/E as a tool for comparison across all companies and all business types. Just a look at all the sectors will show that the P/E varies considerably depending on the type of business being carried on. Water is not likely to push its P/E much above 10, whilst media is likely to be in the late twenties. Water is, of course, a regulated industry whose profits are most unlikely to increase in line with the economic cycle. After a pay rise you are not likely to flush the toilet or bathe more often! A lowly rating of 10 therefore seems as justified for water as the stratospheric P/Es for such shooting stars as Microsoft and the rest of the high technology sector. When will it all end?

## Price earnings – valuation tool

*Key Management Concept*

The real usage of P/Es for unquoted companies is when they are used for valuation purposes. For instance, if you were to own a food retailing business and wanted to sell out to one of the major players, how would you value yourself? Quite simple, really – use the P/E ratio of the acquiring company. If we assume that the acquirer's P/E is around 20, and that your business's profit after tax is £1m, then we could value you at 20 times £1m, or £20m. The problem comes when the purchaser, as they will inevitably do, tries to reduce the P/E of 20. They say that your management is short of the mark, the business is geographically limited and so on – would a P/E of 10 be acceptable? And so the debate continues; this is called the science of valuing a business.

Back to the P/E of quoted companies, and in much the same way that there is an average for each sector, so there is an average for each country. Turning to the pages at the back of section two of the FT you will find an abbreviated version of the stockmarkets of leading industrialised nations. US P/Es are currently higher than ours in the UK, whilst the Japanese average P/E has always frightened the life out of us in the West – often double that of a similar UK business.

Sometimes of course there are anomalies – generally brought about by the mathematics involved. For example, if you make a loss, there will be no P/E shown; the figure simply cannot be computed meaningfully as a negative item. Equally, if profits have been miniscule but the share price has not yet collapsed proportionately, then the P/E can look strangely high for a business in such dire straits. The word of warning is simply that which applies to all financial analysis – be aware that you have all the facts and trends at your fingertips, and don't rely too much on just one measure.

*Key Management Concept*

## Yield gross

On to the second of these two key ratios; yield gross. Whilst this is not quite as important to the man in the street, it does say a lot about a company, subject to the usual caveats above. We simply express the dividend each share receives (as disclosed in the latest financial statements) as a percentage of the current share price. This is broadly the equivalent of saying how much do we get by way of return on every pound invested in shares of that company, and is directly comparable to a bank account or building society account yield – in principle, if not in rate.

We have one further hoop to jump through, though. What we have expressed so far (dividend divided by share price) gives a net yield (as all dividends are physically received net of tax at the appropriate rate). And yet, someone has decided that the yield is better expressed in gross terms, rather than net – so we have to multiply up (gross up) by 100 over 80 to get the gross yield.

Typically, yields in the UK are somewhere between 2% and 6%, hardly stunning when you think what you can get in a bank or building society, and that is risk free. However, as an investor you are probably more concerned by the value of the capital you will hopefully generate, and dividend yield doesn't measure that.

Read through any sector you like, and try to spot the correlation between performance of company (perhaps as evidenced by P/E) and the dividend yield paid. Is there a correlation? If you think there is, then does the direction of the correlation surprise you? Most people would say, unthinkingly, that a higher yield sounds better than a lower yield. On further reflection, though, you should be asking the question 'Why is the business offering a high yield?'. The answer lies in the age old financial truth that 'Low risk equals low reward. High risk equals high reward'. It is quite likely that the low P/E companies will have seemingly attractive high yields, in order to attract investors, whilst the ship itself may be sinking.

So, all in all, a stronger company will probably have a higher P/E and a lower yield than a weaker company. Now is the time to see how your business (or your competitor, customer or supplier) stacks up against the rest, and draw whatever conclusions you may wish.

## Gilts and interest rates

If all this has whetted your appetite for keeping yourself up to date with what is happening in corporate equities in the UK and overseas, then don't forget the complementary side – bonds, or interest bearing debt. To get a feel of what happens here, turn to the page of the *Financial Times* with details of UK government debt (gilts). You will find them occupying about an eighth of a page some six to ten pages from the back of section two.

You can see that gilts are blocked up into several sections – shorts, mediums, longs, undated and index linked. For an explanation of how they work, look at the undated section. Find the first item in the undateds, typically this will be 4% Consols. The next item is $3^1/_2$% War Loan. Neither of these sound as if they are going to set the world on fire in terms of attractive yielding interest rates. However, there is a twist to all this. You should be able to see a column that refers to the current market price of the gilt. Typically the 4% Consols will be somewhere in the range 40p-60p for each item, sometimes written as £40-£60 per £100 nominal (but it means the same thing). Assume that the price is actually 50p; this would mean that you only have to spend 50p in order to get the stated interest of 4p – making the actual yield obtained on the gilt as 4p/50p, or 8%. That sounds more realistic, and you should be able to see a column marked yield showing you exactly this. These gilts are relatively cheaply tradeable, many of them being available through the post office!

*Key Learning Point*

The major point to appreciate here is that this yield on undated gilts is about the market's best estimate of long-term interest rates. What happens therefore, is that the value of a gilt goes down (and yield goes up) when interest rates rise, whilst the value of a gilt goes up (and yield goes down) when interest rates fall. So, where is the risk? Since there is no risk that the UK government will go belly-up, the risk is all in the market's estimate of future interest rates, and therefore the market value of the gilt. Inherently these are some of the few low risk investments that organisations such as banks and insurance companies are allowed to hold (equities can of course always fail completely).

That's about it for our quick run through. You must always remember that the *Financial Times* prides itself on being responsive to reader's needs, with the inevitable consequence that it does change what it reports, and the measure that it uses.

# Review of accounting principles

Chapter 4

## Introduction

This is only be a brief overview of all the complexities that do in fact exist for accountants. Should you have further technical queries please refer to more detailed technical texts, GAAP Statements or Auditing Standards and Guidelines.

## Fixed assets and depreciation

There are two accounting principles associated with fixed assets: the historical cost principle and the matching principle. On the balance sheet we record acquisition of assets at cost. This is called capitalising the cost. The opposite is called expensing, which means we write off the cost of the item through the year's profit and loss account by calling it a revenue cost of that year. Then on the profit and loss account we match the fixed asset cost with revenues over a period of years, using the accrual or matching principle. The method by which asset cost is matched with revenue is depreciation, a technique for spreading the cost of the asset over its useful economic life (the period during which it supports production of revenue in the operating cycle).

*Key Learning Point*

## Carrying cost

When a building or piece of equipment is acquired, there is normally an exchange of cash (or other asset) for it and the cost of the fixed asset is capitalised. It is shown at full value on the balance sheet, rather than listed as an expense on the profit and loss account. The value entered for the asset at the time of purchase is known as the historical cost of the asset. This cost is extremely important because it will always be the figure on the company's balance sheet, regardless of the current resale value, less depreciation. Historical cost is also the value the company uses in allocating the cost of the fixed asset (depreciating).

The cost of fixed assets should include both the direct acquisition cost and related costs for transportation of equipment to its permanent location, site preparation at the location, and any improvements made to the asset.

One test of whether work done on plant and equipment should be treated as a revenue cost or as a capital cost is whether the work substantially increases its value/capacity/quality, or prolongs its useful life. If so, it is treated as a capital expenditure and included in cost on the balance sheet. If not, it is treated as routine maintenance and repair and is included in current expenses.

Whilst SSAP 12 on Accounting for Depreciation allows cost to be historical cost, it encourages revaluations of fixed assets on the grounds that they give 'useful and relevant information to the users of accounts'. Over the years it has become increasingly common for enterprises to revalue their fixed assets (particularly freehold and leasehold property). Where this happens, depreciation must be provided on the revalued amount.

## Depreciation period

Once cost has been established, it is necessary to choose a depreciation period – a time over which the original cost of the asset is to be allocated. Depreciation is defined as 'the measure of wearing out, consumption or other reduction in the useful economic life'.

*Key Learning Point*

The useful economic life of an asset is the period over which the present owner will derive economic benefits from its use, and is usually determined by considering the estimated time of physical and economic deterioration of the asset.

Estimates of economic deterioration are much more subjective, particularly in industries in which frequent technological breakthroughs tend to make older equipment obsolete or uneconomical for the current owner. Whilst the rules do not expect businesses to depreciate land, they do indicate that property should be depreciated. In recent years, however, several industries have not depreciated buildings on the grounds that the buildings are fully maintained and repaired.

## Residual value

Residual value is the realisable value of the asset at the end of its useful economic life, based on prices prevailing at the date of acquisition (or revaluation, if this has taken place). Realisation costs should be deducted in arriving at the residual value.

## Depreciation methods

There are several depreciation methods currently in use, and management should select the method regarded as most appropriate to the type of asset and its use in the business, so as to allocate depreciation as fairly as possible to the periods expected to benefit from the asset's use. Although the straight line method is the simplest to apply, it may not always be the most appropriate.

Depreciation methods are:

- Straight line
- Production or use
- Accelerated methods
  - Reducing balance
  - Sum of digits
- Other specialised methods (e.g. Annuity).

In the first two methods, straight line and production or use, the asset's cost is allocated in roughly equal instalments over the asset's useful life. In reducing balance, the asset's book value is allocated in unequal instalments over the asset's useful life, with larger instalments recognised in the early portion of the useful life and smaller instalments recognised in the later portion.

## Straight line depreciation

Straight line depreciation is the simplest form of depreciation to compute. It is calculated by dividing the cost of the asset, less any estimated residual value, by the estimated number of years in the asset's useful economic life. The resulting figure is recognised as depreciation expense during every year of the asset's useful life.

## Production or use method

The production or use method is similar to the straight-line method except that some unit of measure other than time is used to allocate the cost of the asset over its useful life. For example, a car might be depreciated on the basis of mileage, with a certain portion of its cost allocated to every thousand miles driven. Because the mileage driven might vary from year to year, the annual depreciation allocation might change, but the cost per mile would stay the same.

Suppose that a company purchases a delivery lorry for £15,000. The truck has a 50,000 mile life expectancy. Residual value is expected to be zero.

| | |
|---|---|
| Cost | £ 15,000 |
| Less: Residual value | 0 |
| Equals: Depreciation basis | £ 15,000 |
| Annual depreciation | £15,000 ÷ 50,000 miles = 30p per mile |

## Accelerated depreciation methods

Accelerated depreciation methods assign a higher amount of depreciation in the earlier years of ownership of an asset and a smaller amount each year as the asset ages. Reducing balance is the most widely used accelerated depreciation method.

Under the reducing balance method, depreciation expense is calculated by multiplying the net book value of an asset at the beginning of the year (without making any adjustment for the residual value) by a fixed percentage. Since net book value declines from year to year as the depreciation charge is deducted from the original cost, the fixed percentage results in a smaller charge for depreciation each year.

With this method the carrying value of the asset is never completely written off. The argument in favour of this method is that it allies the depreciation charge to the costs of maintaining and running the asset; in early years these costs are low and the depreciation high, while in later years this is reversed.

The sum of digits is another form of reducing balance. If an asset has a life of four years then the digits 1, 2, 3 and 4 are added together, giving a total of 10. Depreciation of 4/10ths, 3/10ths, 2/10ths and 1/10th is charged in each year.

Other methods used are chosen by each business to more fairly reflect the particular circumstances affecting their particular fixed assets. The annuity method, for example, is based on 'the cost of capital notionally invested in the asset'.

## Depreciation for tax purposes

*Key Learning Point*

Perhaps the most important fact to realise about business tax generally is that the Inland Revenue have their own set of rules for computing what is allowable for tax purposes, and that often the accounting profit reported in the profit and loss account bears little resemblance to the taxable profit.

As you have seen so far, the choice of depreciation rate and amount is wholly subjective, and effectively the accounting profit reflects the management's subjectivity.

Understandably this degree of freedom (and the ability to 'manipulate' profits) is not supported by the Inland Revenue, whose view is that capital expenditure is not an allowable deduction in arriving at taxable profit. Instead, the Revenue have created their own recognised rates of tax allowances that replace depreciation – called Capital Allowances.

## Expenditure eligible for allowances

There is a wide and complex set of definitions for eligible expenditure, but the important ones include:

- Machinery and plant (includes cars, computers etc.)
- Industrial buildings
- Agricultural buildings
- Scientific research and patent rights
- Mineral extraction, dredging.

More important is the fact that certain expenditure, which is clearly capital for business purposes, is simply not allowable; the main one being expenditure on non-industrial property and buildings.

## Rates of capital allowances

There are several rates for capital allowances, but the Writing Down Allowance of 25% reducing balance is the cornerstone and is generally applicable to the majority of everyday assets.

Other allowances either relate to different annual percentage rates, or are rates applicable to the first year of expenditure (Initial, or First Year Allowances).

What this means in practice, therefore, is that businesses often depreciate in financial statements at a different rate to the tax allowances awarded by the Revenue. Although this rarely causes problems, we will discuss the implications of this later.

## Property

Most fixed assets (including buildings) have an identifiable useful life after which it either wears out or becomes obsolete; the expense of purchasing it is therefore depreciated. However, land has an indefinite or infinite useful life and therefore is not depreciated. Land carried on a balance sheet can result in unrecognised income or gains (the appreciation in the market value of land that is not recognised in the profit and loss account until the land is sold). The balance sheet may well give you a very conservative view of the value of assets such as land. Their cost may be substantially lower than the price at which they could be sold. Always try to determine the current market value of land as well as any carrying costs associated with land.

# Long-term liabilities

In the long-term portion of the balance sheet liabilities section, you'll normally find three items: deferred tax (not tax at all, but a technical accounting provision), long-term debt, and commitments and contingencies.

## Long-term debt

Property, plant and equipment are the physical assets a company uses over several years or accounting periods to produce or support production of the goods and services it sells. A company should have a long-term source for financing purchase of these assets; otherwise, it risks serious cash shortages resulting from payment for a long-lived asset from operating cycle cash before the asset generates enough profits to repay the loan. You should always be alert to this mismatching, which occurs when a company uses short-term debt to finance long-term assets.

Normally, to avoid this companies finance their long-term assets with the owners' equity in the business or with long-term loans. Companies' long-term debt normally is one of three types:

- Long-term leases
- Long-term bank debt
- Other long-term debt.

## Long-term leases

When a company enters into a contract to lease, it agrees to rent fixed assets (normally land, buildings or equipment) for a specified period of time.

The company using the asset is called the lessee; the company that owns the asset is called the lessor. The lessee agrees to make periodic payments (for example, monthly, quarterly, or annually) to the lessor in return for use of the asset. At the end of the lease, the lessee returns the asset to its owner. The lease contract creates an obligation for the lessee to make payments in much the same way as a bank loan agreement; in effect, it is long-term financing of the asset that is attractive because of certain tax advantages to the lessee and possibly the lessor, depending on the terms of the lease agreement.

The rules governing the accounting treatment for leases are contained in SSAP 21 *Accounting for Leases and Hire Purchase Contracts*. This standard was one of the most controversial at the time of its issue in 1984, as it effectively invoked a 'substance over form' approach. In other words in spite of never actually owning a leased asset, accountants would now insist that sometimes the asset would be included on the balance sheet as if it were owned.

According to SSAP 21 the accounting treatment depends on the type of lease. From the standpoint of the lessee, there are two types of leases: finance leases and operating leases.

A finance lease is classified as a 'lease which transfers substantially all the risks and rewards of ownership of an asset to the lessee'; whilst an operating lease is a 'lease other than a finance lease'.

So how do we define the '...substantially all...' part? There is one significant definition that indicates a finance lease; otherwise the lease is an operating one:

> 'The present value of the minimum lease payments (discounted at the lease rate of interest) equals or exceeds 90 percent of the fair value of the leased property at the start of the lease.'

Computers, office copying machines, automobiles and lorries are the primary types of assets covered by operating leases. The lease contract is frequently written for considerably less than the expected life of the asset leased.

SSAP 21 sets out accounting requirements for both operating leases and finance leases. The treatment of operating leases is simple: the annual payment is listed as a rental expense on the profit and loss account, and details of the lease together with future commitments are usually provided in a note to the accounts. Finance leases are less simple. The rules say that capitalised leases should be shown on the balance sheet as if the company had purchased the equipment, because the company is in effect getting virtually all of the use of that asset. The company's financial statements will show interest, depreciation, and an asset and liability for the capitalised lease as though the leased asset were purchased and financed with regular long-term debt.

The amount to be capitalised is not the fair value of the asset, but the present value (PV) of the minimum lease payments. For hire purchase agreements the capitalised amount should be depreciated over the useful life of the asset, and for finance leases over the lease term if that is shorter.

The net amount of the obligations under finance leases should be analysed between the amounts payable within one year, two to five years and thereafter. The aggregate finance charges for the period for finance leases should also be disclosed. Be aware that disclosure of leases in the financial statements can signal a significant use of a company's cash.

## Leasing

Leasing is a classic example of where the accounting rules bear little resemblance to reality. We all know that leased assets technically never belong to the user of the asset. If I lease a car, for example, I never actually legally own that car.

*Key Learning Point*

Certain events in the recent past, however, have caused accountants to sit up and take a radically different view – a view that is seen as being either helpful (according to some) or potentially dangerous (according to others).

Let's look back at one particular example of an airline which went out of business in the 1970s. Its greatest apparent asset, as you would expect for an airline, was of course the aircraft themselves. But they leased them all, so you wouldn't expect to find anything on the balance sheet. And you didn't. So, all the equity shareholders queued up to await their anticipated handout of so many pence in the pound… only to become distraught when told that there wouldn't be a payout owing to the large amount of contractual debt that the beleaguered company owed in respect of the aircraft it had leased. In other words, the assets weren't on the balance sheet – but then neither was the debt. And the debt didn't want to go away.

This wasn't the first occurrence of 'off balance sheet debt', and it certainly won't be the last. But it was the last straw that broke the camel's back. The camel, in the form of the accounting standard setting body, invented a standard that is still very much with us today in spirit, although its precise application may have been tempered with later pronouncements.

What was invented was an accounting standard for leasing and hire purchase which broke new ground due to its acceptance of the 'substance over form' principle. Simply because you didn't actually own an asset, under certain circumstances you might well have to include the asset (and, of course, the corresponding debt) in the balance sheet. All this was invoked, quite fairly, as being for the overall benefit of the reader of financial statements, as well as giving a fairer and more informative picture of a company's financial health.

We split leases into two quite distinct (from an accountant's point of view types: finance and operating leases.

Let's be quite clear about operating leases. These are the ones that don't cause any trouble – they are just treated as if the asset is being rented. In other words, the annual lease payment is treated as rental, and the full amount is treated as a revenue expense in the profit and loss account.

Finance leases are defined as being those leases where more than 90% of the initial value of the asset is consumed during the life of that lease. This is simply a yardstick that was believed to be sufficient to catch those items where in reality, this definition means that longer term bigger ticket items are likely to be caught, whilst short-term assets will escape.

So, the lease that causes a problem is the finance lease. These are the ones where, broadly, the fair value of the asset is brought on the balance sheet as a fixed asset. An approximately equal but opposite amount is shown on the balance sheet in liabilities (split between short and long-term, as appropriate).

Now there are obviously technical issues beyond the scope of this book, but the following might be a good example of how it might look.

Let's take an asset whose cash cost is £10,000. We can buy it under a finance lease for annual payments of £3,000. The total cost under the leasing route is a total of four times £3,000, or £12,000. Since the cash cost was £10,000, we deduce that the difference of £2,000 is due to the interest charged. Assuming that we are justified in spreading the interest evenly across the life of the repayments (four years), we infer that annual interest is some £500. So, each annual installment is made up of £2,500 of capital repayment and £500 of interest.

If we assume that the asset falls within the scope and definition of a finance lease as defined above, we can now set about including the asset (and corresponding liability) in the approved manner.

### Step 1

Firstly, let's deal with putting the asset in the balance sheet. We should include £10,000 within fixed assets (plant and machinery, motor vehicles or wherever appropriate). Sadly, our balance sheet is now out of balance. We need to put £10,000 in the liability sections, but which ones? Assuming that our capital and interest repayments are evenly spread (as discussed above), there should be £2,500 in current liabilities (due for payment within the next 12 months) and £7,500 in long-term liabilities (repayments due in years 2, 3 and 4). Now the balance sheet balances.

What about the other parts of the transaction? There are two more parts: depreciation and interest.

### Step 2

Since there is a new fixed asset, we will have to depreciate it. Four years sounds like a sensible depreciation life, which gives an amount of £2,500 per annum. This amount will be an expense in the profit and loss account, and will reduce the net book value of the asset in the balance sheet.

### Step 3

The interest of £500 per annum needs to be charged to the profit and loss account.

### Step 4

Finally we actually make the annual payment of £3,000 to the leasing company. Cash reduces by £3,000, but so does the liability to the leasing company. Back to all square.

## Balance sheet

| | Operating lease | Finance lease | | | | | | |
|---|---|---|---|---|---|---|---|---|
| | | Step 1 | Step 2 | After 2 | Step 3 | After 3 | Step 4 | After 4 |
| *Fixed assets* | | | | | | | | |
| Plant and machinery | | £10,000 | -£2,500 | £7,500 | | £7,500 | -£3,000 | £7,500 |
| *Current assets* | | | | | | | | |
| Cash | -£3,000 | | | | | -£3,000 | | -3,000 |
| *Current liabilities* | | | | | | | | |
| Amounts owed to lease company | | 2,500 | | 2,500 | 500 | 3,000 | -500 | 2,500 |
| *Long term liabilities* | | | | | | | | |
| Amounts owed to lease company | | 7,500 | | 7,500 | | 7,500 | -2,500 | 5,000 |
| net effect | -£3,000 | £0 | -£2,500 | -£2,500 | -£500 | -£3,000 | £0 | -£3,000 |

## Profit and loss account

| | Operating lease | Finance lease | | | | | | |
|---|---|---|---|---|---|---|---|---|
| | | Step 1 | Step 2 | After 2 | Step 3 | After 3 | Step 4 | After 4 |
| Interest | | | | | £500 | £500 | | £500 |
| Depreciation | | | £2,500 | £2,500 | | 2,500 | | 2,500 |
| Lease payments | £3,000 | | | | | | | |
| net effect | -£3,000 | £0 | -£2,500 | -£2,500 | -£500 | -£3,000 | £0 | -£3,000 |

| | |
|---|---|
| Payments | 4 |
| Amount | 3,000 |
| Lease price | 12,000 |
| Cash price | 10,000 |
| Interest | 2,000 |
| Annual interest | 500 |
| Depreciation | 2,500 |

In fact, you can see that the overall effect of the operating vs. finance lease treatment is this: in both cases the profit and loss account is hit with the same expense (albeit under different names), whilst the balance sheet shows no net increase (merely a 'grossing up' of asset and debt in the finance lease case). It's really quite a neat way to get the asset and debt 'on balance sheet'.

There is obviously more to the whole matter of leasing than we have had time to cover here, indeed it is a whole industry in itself. Designing contracts, assets, lives and residual values to be or not to be a finance rather than operating lease – not forgetting dovetailing in with the best possible tax advantage.

## Sale and leaseback

You may hear or see references to sale and leaseback arrangements. Sale and leaseback is a form of financing. A company sells its office building, for example, and leases back the space. The company is trading a short-term inflow of cash for a long-term outflow of cash. The profit and loss on a sale and leaseback should be accounted for in different ways, depending on whether it is a finance or operating lease.

Finally, the whole of the leasing debate has seemingly been influenced by the recently introduced FRS 5 *Reporting the Substance of Transactions,* reinforcing the principle of 'substance over form'. It deals with many of the issues covered specifically by SSAP 21, sometimes differently, but it does state clearly that for the moment SSAP 21 is still to be used for leasing.

## Other long-term debt

Other long-term debt is the wide variety of loan capital raised via capital markets and includes debenture stock, unsecured loan stock and convertible loan stock. They are long-term legal obligations or contracts that a company issues to institutional investors (such as insurance companies) or to the general public in return for cash. More simply put, they are long-term IOUs the company sells as a way of borrowing money. Companies use them to borrow for periods as long as 30 years, a much longer period than a typical bank loan.

When a company sells a bond (borrows money), it issues a certificate containing a promise to repay the sum of money borrowed at a specific date or dates in the future. The amount of money the company is obligated to repay is called the face value or par value, and the timetable for repaying that money is called the repayment schedule. In addition, the company promises to pay a fixed amount of interest on a regular basis to the buyer of the bond, with payment usually scheduled every six months, irrespective of the company's profitability. Interest is an allowable expense for tax, making debt capital more efficient than dividends on equity capital. The interest rate (for example, 10 percent) used to calculate this fixed amount of interest is known as the bond's coupon.

When a company issues loan capital it can offer some security with it (debenture stock) or not (unsecured loan stock). A debenture is normally secured by a fixed and/or floating charge on specific identifiable assets, and also specifies the legal provisions of the debt, such as due date and interest rate. A third party, called the trustee, is usually appointed to represent the debenture holders and to ensure that the issuer fulfils all the terms of the deed.

There are specific provisions in the deed that the issuer (borrower) agrees to, of which the most important is the issuer agreeing to repay the face value of the stock at some point in the future, and to pay certain amounts of interest. However, there are other items that will be very important to you. For example, some clauses limit the amount of bank debt the company can take on. Other clauses require that all future debt added by the company be subordinate to this issue, in other words, payment of this stock would take precedence over payment of any future debt.

Unsecured loan stock will rank equally with other unsecured creditors in the event of a liquidation, behind debenture holders and preferential creditors (tax, business rates and certain employee obligations).

There are many different kinds of debt. Some may contain provisions that allow the holder to convert to other securities, such as the company's ordinary or preference shares. This is normally called convertible unsecured loan stock, or CULS. A convertible is attractive for the following reasons:

- For the company, the coupon is generally much lower than a straight-forward unsecured loan stock.

- For the company, the loan is cheaper to service than equity.

- For the investor, it provides income with a certain degree of capital security.

## Discounts, premiums and cash flow

Generally, loan stock is not sold at face value, which means that you will often see references to profits and losses on issues not made at par, and the expenses of issuing, being normally taken direct to reserves.

Since it is impossible to predetermine the exact interest rate that will prevail in the market for debt that is being offered with similar risk, ratings and terms, the stock usually sells either above or below face value; that is, at a premium or a discount. If interest rates are higher than the coupon rate, the bond is sold at a discount, giving investors a yield that is comparable to other securities on the market; if the interest rates are lower than the coupon rate, the bond is sold at a premium.

## Deep discounts

Some companies issue loan capital at a substantial discount (15%) to the par value, to reduce the coupon. Investors are attracted because, although the interest is negligible or nil, the capital gain on redemption is large.

## Sinking funds

A sinking fund is a separate cash fund built up over the life of the debt that is used to pay off the face amount of debt as they mature. A sinking fund provides assurance to investors that money will be available to pay off their debts when they mature; it also provides the company with a means of setting aside the cash to pay off long-term debt on a regular basis over the lifetime of the debt rather than all at one time. Payments to a sinking fund have the same effect on cash flow and the balance sheet as other debt repayments.

## Warrants

Warrants are long-term options granted by the company, entitling holders to subscribe for ordinary shares during some future period at some specified price. Warrants are issued with debt to make them more attractive to the investor, particularly when the company is reluctant to issue straightforward loan capital (for example when interest rates are high) or when investors are reluctant to purchase fixed interest securities.

If the company performs well, the warrants will yield a valuable return. Warrants are normally detachable and are exercisable once the exercise price is reached, but they will seldom be exercised until close to the final exercise date since investors want to maximise their gearing.

## Notes, loan notes and commercial paper

Notes and loan notes are promissory notes issued to one, or a small number, of companies or individuals. They are generally between one and ten years' maturity. Commercial paper is a negotiable unsecured promissory note, and forms a short-term loan vehicle.

## Bonds

Bonds are the generic name for any loan capital raised through the Eurobond or domestic markets. The amounts may be denominated in sterling or in any foreign currency.

## Mezzanine finance

This is a term describing finance that lies between 'straight' debt and share capital, often used where the total debt is restricted (e.g. Management Buy Out). It will often be a loan that ranks after the normal/senior debt, and to compensate will have a higher rate of interest and options to convert to equity (or warrants).

The permutations for debt capital are almost endless. The great corporate finance period of the 1980's generated many hybrids such as junk bonds, which baffled lenders and analysts for some time; the next period of activity will be no different.

## Provisions and estimated liabilities

Provisions and estimated liabilities are obligations that definitely will have to be paid but for which the amount and timing are uncertain. They are reported on the balance sheet, and the methods used to estimate them, along with other disclosures required by GAAP, are included in notes to the accounts.

## Provisions

Typically the commonest provisions are those for:

- Pensions and similar obligations

- Taxation, including deferred taxation

- Other provisions.

## Pensions

Before SSAP 24 *Accounting for Pension Costs* was introduced in 1988 pension costs were charged to the profit and loss account on the basis of funding payments made. This meant that the company's profits could fluctuate from year to year, depending on contributions, and little information was given about the assets or the obligations for the scheme.

Since SSAP 24 the measure of pension cost is no longer simply what it was. Instead the figure is now derived directly from the actuarial valuations of the scheme. In effect, the fund is treated as a company asset, even if it is not shown directly on the balance sheet.

There is currently considerable debate about amendments to the standard, including the underlying philosophy adopted by SSAP 24.

## Commitments

The rules require that the aggregate amounts of the following be shown by way of a note to the accounts:

- Contracts for capital expenditure (not already provided for).

- Capital expenditure authorised by directors, which has not been contracted for.

The note can give some indication of the extent to which the directors plan to expand the facilities of the business, and the likely impact on future cash flows.

## Contingent liabilities

A contingent liability is a potential liability that had not materialised by the date of the balance sheet. The rules (SSAP 18) state that a note to the accounts must be prepared detailing the potential liability. In many cases notes are of no real significance, since no liability is anticipated, nor arises.

The contingencies here are not usual, but they would not affect the company's ability to continue operating. Any decisions you might have to make on the basis of the financial statements should take such a contingency into consideration. The accountants don't always tell you how to evaluate the information; they just signal the situation.

Some notes signal serious situations: product liability under pending class action suits; litigation resulting from breach of securities or other laws; major civil or criminal liability for negligence; or potential loss of production facilities because of nationalisation by foreign governments. In addition, liability for major chemical spills or pollution clean-up might appear as a contingency, as would major suits for breach of contract, patent or copyright infringement, violation of antitrust laws, or other activities that would have a material (and usually adverse) effect on the company's financial condition.

# Owners' equity in companies

There are usually three major headings in the owners' equity section of corporate balance sheets, and are often referred to as shareholders' funds:

- Share capital: typically ordinary and preference shares.

- Retained earnings or the cumulative profit and loss account.

- Other reserves, such as share premium and revaluation reserve.

## Ordinary shares: basic concepts

The ordinary shareholders, in theory, exercise the ultimate control and ownership of a company. They elect (through a voting process) a board of directors to oversee the management of the company. The board of directors usually has the authority to choose the senior officers of the company: the chairman, for example. In most companies the preference shareholders do not vote to elect the board of directors.

*Key Management Concept*

Ordinary shareholders are the beneficiaries of a company's success and growth in earnings. At the same time, ordinary shareholders are the most vulnerable if the business fails. If the business is profitable, with profits left after payment of all obligations to suppliers, banks, debenture holders and preference shareholders, then the ordinary shareholders benefit. If the business is unprofitable and the company is liquidated with no proceeds from the sale of assets left after all obligations are paid, then the ordinary shareholders lose their investment. A shareholder's liability for the company's debts is limited to his or her investment in the company: a shareholder who invested £100 can lose no more than £100 when the company is liquidated, regardless of the company's debts.

## Preference shares: basic concepts

While rewards to the ordinary shareholders are generally directly tied to the uncertain success and growth of the company, owners of preference shares normally are entitled to their rewards. Generally, preference shareholders are entitled to priority over ordinary shareholders in receiving a return on their investment (for example, dividends) while the business is a going concern. The preference shareholders are also entitled to priority in the return of their investment when the business is liquidated. This preference in receiving dividends and in repayment of investment is the reason that the shares have acquired their name. Preference share dividends represent a mandatory use of funds for a company. Normally preference shares dividends are not delayed or deferred if cash is a little tight.

Even though preference shares have some advantages over ordinary shares in terms of dividends and priority on liquidation, preference shares also have some disadvantages. Usually the amount of dividends on preference shares is fixed. For example, take a preference share with an annual fixed dividend of £1 per share. If the business is very profitable, the owners of ordinary shares might receive dividends of £2 or £3 a share, rather than the £1 paid to the owner of preference shares, even though the price of the preference share and the ordinary share may have been the same when they were issued. On the other hand, if the company's net income is too low to pay both ordinary and preference dividends, the owner of the preference share could receive £1 while the owner of the ordinary share receives nothing.

In addition to the dividend limitation, the owners of preference shares normally are restricted in their participation in the management of the business. The owners, or shareholders, of a company normally participate in management by electing a board of directors who in turn select the managers of the company. The voting rights of preference shareholders, however, are often restricted so that these shareholders either have no right to vote or are restricted to electing directors only when their dividend payments have been missed. The rights of a preference shareholder are spelled out in corporate documents such as memorandum and articles of association, as well as in the preference shares certificates.

## Ordinary shares: technical terms

The amount of ordinary shares a company has is determined by its legal documents: memorandum and articles of association, and subsequent resolutions by its board of directors. The total number of ordinary shares that a company is permitted to have is called its authorised share capital. This amount may be the same as or more than the number of shares that it has issued, or sold, to the investing public. The type and nominal amount of each share must be stated. For example, a company may be authorised to issue 100,000 £1 ordinary shares, but may choose to sell only 55,000 £1 ordinary shares. The remaining 45,000 £1 ordinary shares are said to be authorised but unissued and can be issued, or sold, at a later date.

The nominal value has little economic significance, but it does have some legal significance because the legislation which governs incorporation usually defines nominal value as the minimum cushion of owners' equity required by law to protect creditors against losses by the business, the concept of the creditors' buffer. Generally, shareholders are not permitted to withdraw this amount through dividends.

## Share premium account

The nominal value is normally substantially lower than the price for which the company plans to sell the shares. The difference between the nominal value assigned to the shares and the price at which the shares are actually sold, or issued, is called a share premium and is not available for distribution as dividends (a non-distributable reserve). For example, if a company assigns a nominal value of £10 per share and sells the shares for £100 each, the premium would be £90 per share.

Cash received from the sale of shares increases both the company's assets (for example, cash) and the amount of shareholders' funds.

Sometimes, as in a stock dividend or a shares split, companies issue additional ordinary shares to their shareholders by capitalising the share premium account. Shareholders therefore do not pay cash for them.

## Stock dividend

In a stock dividend the company gives the shareholders a dividend in the form of additional shares of shares, rather than paying out cash. This is popular with the company because it raises extra capital without expenses, and popular with investors since they can add shares without commission costs.

## Scrip or bonus issue

A scrip, bonus or capitalisation issue is a free issue of additional new shares to existing shareholders, and is made by capitalising reserves.

## Share splits

In a share split additional shares are created; the company hopes to make shares more marketable by reducing or splitting the price of each individual share. There is no transfer between the different shareholders' funds accounts. The only change is that the nominal value per share (and hopefully the market value) is adjusted to reflect the new shares.

## Rights issue

A rights issue is an issue of new shares at a discount to market value, offered to existing shareholders. The discount is measured to be attractive to purchasers, but not so great as to drive down the market value of shares in existence.

## Share options

A company may also give its managers the opportunity to buy its shares in the future at a fixed price. This right to buy shares at a fixed price is known as a share option.

Normally, the option fixes the price so that the company's management has an incentive to manage the company well and make it profitable. The expectation is that the share price will rise above the option's fixed price and the managers will make a profit by selling the shares acquired with the option.

## Retained earnings

If a business is profitable, the ordinary shareholders' ownership interest is increased by the profits. Some of these profits are normally paid out in dividends to the ordinary shareholders and some are kept in the business to provide capital for further expansion. The amount kept in the business (the difference between the net income that belongs to the ordinary shareholders and the cash dividends paid to them) is known as retained earnings and is shown in the owners' equity section of the balance sheet.

The combination of the shares and the retained earnings accounts represents the capital, or the ownership interests, of the shareholders (the ultimate owners of the company). Bankers and investors often refer to the sum of the shares and the retained earnings accounts as the balance sheet total or net worth, the difference between all assets at their balance sheet carrying value and all liabilities.

## Revaluation reserve

When certain fixed assets are revalued the asset is shown at more (rarely less) than the historical cost, so what do we do with the difference in order to make the accounts balance?

The answer is to add the revaluation surplus to the revaluation reserve; this is not distributable until such time as the asset is sold and the surplus realised.

## Other reserves

Other reserves may include reserves for capital redemption (to do with redemption of preference or ordinary shares), consolidation items, or foreign currency fluctuations. Their technical aspects are somewhat difficult, and are not discussed here.

# Notes to the accounts

## Overview

In recent years, a pronounced emphasis has been placed on the need for full disclosure by the accounting profession. Although full disclosure has always been a basic principle on which financial statements have been prepared and auditors' opinions rendered, a spate of litigation in recent years has brought this issue to the forefront. Plaintiffs have been awarded large settlements to compensate them for bad investment decisions. These decisions were based on a review of financial statements that did not fully disclose or properly represent a company's true financial condition.

*Key Learning Point*

Banks have also initiated litigation and have won judgements from a borrower's management as well as their auditors. Typically, these cases involved loans that could not be collected, that were extended on the basis of financial information that later proved to be incomplete or inaccurate.

The difficulty for the accounting profession is the definition of what constitutes full disclosure. Full disclosure is commonly defined as the provision of sufficient information to allow the average investor to make a knowledgeable decision about the financial standing of a company. Obviously, this definition is open to different interpretations.

*Key Learning Point*

In recent years, the Financial Reporting Council (FRC) and the Accounting Standards Board (ASB) have given more stringent specifications of what constitutes full disclosure. Financial statements generally consist of a balance sheet, profit and loss account, cash flow statement, various other specialised financial reports and notes to the accounts. Because the statements and reports are limited in the amount of information they can contain, the additional information needed to comply with full disclosure requirements has expanded the notes to the accounts.

## Annual report and accounts

A typical public company's annual report and accounts would contain the following major statements:

- Directors' report
- Balance sheet
- Profit and loss account
- Cash flow statement
- Notes to the accounts
- Auditors' report on the above items.

Since we have already looked at three of these items, we will now examine the Directors' report, the Notes to the accounts and the Auditors' Report.

## Directors' report

This is supposed to be a standardised report that all companies produce, and unless the information is included elsewhere in the report and accounts, you can reasonably expect the directors' report to include the following:

- Names and details of directors and their shareholdings
- Major areas of business, together with any significant changes
- Changes in fixed assets
- Research and development expenditure
- Review of this year's activities
- Future developments
- Post year end events of importance
- Details of own shares purchased.

## Notes to the accounts

The amount of information that is contained in a company's statements will depend on whether the company is public or private. Private companies are not legally required to adopt full disclosure unless they have sold or are planning to sell securities that are registered with the Stock Exchange. A typical list of items in the notes to the accounts could include the following:

- Accounting policies
- Authorised share capital
- Details of shares and debentures issued
- Transfers to/from reserves
- Fixed asset details – additions, disposals, depreciation
- Turnover and profit by geographical and industry analysis
- Directors' remuneration

- Average number of employees, wages and pension details
- Auditors' fees
- Taxation details
- Foreign currency translation details
- Subsidiaries and associated undertakings
- Ultimate holding company
- Analyses of normal balance sheet accounts – stock, debtors, creditors etc.

The most fundamental requirement in any statement is a disclosure of the accounting methods used to present the major accounts. These notes to the accounts commonly include:

- Methods used to value fixed assets and to calculate depreciation charge and amortisation of intangibles
- Methods of valuing stock
- Details of employee costs
- Description of accounting policy and accounting method changes from those used in previous periods, with an analysis of the effect of the changes.

The directors have different accounting options to choose from within GAAP, each of which can have a significant effect on reported income, profits and balance sheet values. The notes to the accounts should contain sufficient information to reveal how the accounting policy that was chosen affected the reported values.

Other disclosures that are particularly useful to readers of accounts are:

- Terms and conditions of any capital leases
- Contingent liabilities
- Composition of debt structure
- Equity structure
- Contractual liabilities
- Segmental and geographical analysis.

## Stock valuation

Stock is one of the main asset accounts for most wholesale and retail businesses as well as many manufacturing companies. You should understand the true value of a company's stock and how readily that stock converts into debtors or cash when it is sold. It is also critical to assess the company's true operating performance at the gross profit level (sales less the cost of goods sold); the stock valuation policy that is used will influence that picture. Depending on the accounting policy, stock levels on the balance sheet may or may not approximate the true realisable value of the stock in the marketplace.

The distribution of stock between the categories of raw materials, work in progress, and finished goods is given in notes to the accounts. Finished goods are the most liquid kind of stock, and it is probably better to see concentration of the stock in this category. Raw materials usually have a much lower liquidation value, and work in progress stock an even lower value.

## Depreciation and amortisation charge

Notes to the accounts often contain information about the type of depreciation rates that are applied to the company's fixed assets. The annual depreciation or amortisation charge for an asset can provide an indication of the useful life of the asset, which in turn is an indicator of a company's probable future borrowing requirement to replace depleted assets.

## Changes in accounting policy

The most common changes in accounting methods include switches in stock valuation or depreciation rates. Management will often have previous periods restated to allow statements to be easily compared to each another. Although there are usually legitimate reasons for such changes, quite often the result is significant fluctuations in profitability. Scrutinise the rationale for the change, and if possible 'strip away' the impact of the change to see the company's true operating performance.

Certain disclosures and presentation of accounting changes in the financial statements and notes to the accounts require presentation of amounts as though the newly adopted accounting principle had always been used.

## Leases

Many firms use leases as a form of financing to acquire fixed assets rather than purchase those assets directly. Commonly leased assets include transportation equipment, warehouses, and most types of machinery and equipment. The advantage for the company that is acquiring the assets under a lease (the lessee) is that lease agreement terms are often more attractive than loan terms offered by banks. The leasing company (the lessor) can offer better terms because it normally retains ownership of the leased asset, and can claim capital allowances for tax purposes and make use of the residual value of the asset when it is returned at the end of the lease term.

Although the lessor retains ownership of the asset, SSAP 21 in many circumstances requires a lessee to 'capitalise' the leased asset on the balance sheet as if the company had actually purchased it, and to reflect the lease payments as a liability. The standard ensures that a company's balance sheet indicates the cash flow implications of a leasing arrangement.

## Contingent liabilities

These notes to the accounts are used to disclose potential obligations that the company may face in the future, but which are not quantifiable as of the statement date in terms of the exact amount or date on which the payment will be incurred. As a consequence, it is not possible to represent any liability and associated expense on the financial statements. Examples of contingent liabilities include pending litigation, environmental disputes, and other legal claims. The note to the accounts will often contain the amount of the pending claim and a statement by management on whether they believe the claim has merit. Examine these notes to the accounts carefully and consult management to determine, as accurately as possible, the effect the contingent liabilities might have on the firm's financial standing.

## Debt structure

A debt structure note to the accounts typically provides a breakdown of the major elements of the company's debt. These elements could include bank debt, loan stock and private placements. The note to the accounts usually provides the interest rate for each debt, the payment requirements, and the maturity date. It may also disclose whether the debt is secured or unsecured and whether it is senior or subordinated. For short-term and long-term revolving credit facilities, the note to the accounts may indicate the amount of unused borrowing capacity that is available.

If any of the debt instruments contain covenants, such as a minimum working capital requirement, the company's compliance or default may also be disclosed. In the case of both finance and operating leases, future payment obligations are commonly stated. Carefully analyse these notes to the accounts so that you understand the effect of the debt structure on the firm's future liquidity and cash flow.

## Equity structure

An equity structure note to the accounts details for each kind of share, such as ordinary or preference stock:

- the number of shares authorised, issued, and fully paid
- the nominal value of each share
- and the voting rights.

It may also disclose the number of share options outstanding for each kind of security. If the company has convertible stocks or bonds, the note to the accounts may state the kind of equity security and the number of shares that could be purchased in the event that the conversion feature is exercised.

## Contractual liabilities

Examples of contractual liabilities include pension agreements and commitments to purchase third party assets. A note to the accounts usually discloses the amount of the financial obligation that will be incurred as well as the timing of associated payments. In the case of pensions, it is important to scrutinise any gap that exists between funded and unfunded future pension obligations. Leases, as mentioned earlier, typically contain future payment commitments that the firm is contractually bound to honour. Unlike contingent liabilities, contractual liabilities are commitments whose pound amount and timing can be accurately assessed.

## Segmental and geographical analysis

Increasingly, the larger publicly traded corporations are also disclosing in extensive notes to the accounts the breakdown of their operations by major business line, industry, geographic concentration, or other significant segments. This typically involves a list of the major asset, liability, and profit and loss statements that correspond to each segment. This level of disclosure has been recommended in recent years to allow users of the statements to make a more accurate assessment of risk for conglomerates with global operations.

## Other types of notes to the accounts

Any account can have a note to the accounts, if it is required or desirable for full disclosure. Common ones include an employee and directors' remuneration note, a breakdown of major components included in the operating expense total, details of acquisitions, new investments and disposals, and a detailed analysis of the company's tax position.

# GAAP mechanism

## Generally Accepted Accounting Principles

Generally Accepted Accounting Principles (GAAP) are the rules that accountants normally apply in preparing financial information. These rules are not the result of formal legislation; rather, they reflect historical practice and consensus among accountants about the way in which specific transactions should be treated. There may be two or more generally accepted ways of accounting for the same transaction. This is a critical point because financial statements may present different pictures according to the accounting method that was chosen.

In the UK the term GAAP is used more loosely than it is in most other countries, where GAAP has a statutory or regulatory definition or authority.

The historical development of GAAP has its roots in the following key steps:

- The introduction of the 'true and fair' concept in the 1947 Companies Act (previously 'true and correct')

- Statements of Standard Accounting Practice (SSAPs) introduced in 1971 by a committee of accountancy bodies (CCAB), and managed by the Accounting Standards Committee (ASC)

- Financial Reporting Standards (FRSs), which have taken over from SSAPs since 1990, and managed by the Accounting Standards Board (ASB)

- Statements of Recommended Practice (SORPs), now managed by the Accounting Standards Board (ASB)

- Companies Acts 1985 and 1989, and implementation of European Directives

- International Accounting Standards and the drive towards standardisation.

## Organisations that influence GAAP

Several organisations help to define, directly or indirectly, the rules that fall within GAAP. The most important of these organisations are:

- Consultative Committee of Accountancy Bodies (CCAB)

- Financial Reporting Council (FRC)

- Accounting Standards Board (ASB)

- Financial Reporting Review Panel (FRRP)

- Urgent Issues Task Force (UITF)

- The Stock Exchange.

# Auditing principles

## Role of the auditor – accounting firms and services

Accounting firms vary greatly in their size and scope of activity. They range from small, local firms to large international firms with hundreds of partners and thousands of professionals.

Accounting services fall into three categories:

1. **Advice on accounting systems and procedures:** accounting firms help clients design and implement accounting systems that suit their internal and external financial reporting requirements.

2. **Auditing of accounting systems:** accounting firms test accounting systems to ensure they provide the proper checks and balances.

3. **Financial statement review:** accountants review clients' financial statements to ensure that management has treated the underlying accounting transactions in accordance with GAAP.

Audits provide assurances about your customers' financial statements. You will see two main kinds of financial statements: audited and unaudited.

1. Audited statements have been thoroughly analysed by independent auditors and carry a report from the independent auditors regarding the completeness and fairness of the information they summarise.

2. Unaudited statements do not carry opinions regarding their fairness and compliance with GAAP.

## Audited financial statements

When auditors perform audits they do not prepare the financial statements. In this way they are able to maintain their status as independent third parties.

Auditors examine the accounting systems and procedures used in preparing the statements.

They are required to report to the members (shareholders) whether, in their opinion, the financial statements have been properly prepared in accordance with the Companies Acts and all relevant SSAPs and FRSs, and give a true and fair view of the profit and state of affairs of the company. The auditors' report covers the accounts and includes the notes to the accounts and the directors' report (to some degree).

An audit therefore has two main purposes:

1. To determine whether the directors have prepared the financial statements in accordance with GAAP.

2. To ascertain that the statements present fairly what they are supposed to present, with reasonable assurance that they are free of material mis-statements.

The auditor expresses an opinion about the following points:

- Whether the accounting principles comply with GAAP and have been appropriately applied

- Whether the financial statements represent fairly, in all material aspects and in conformity with GAAP, the information contained in the company's financial books and records

- Whether the financial statements and accompanying notes contain all material information necessary for their proper interpretation

- Whether the information in the financial statements (including the notes) reflects the underlying events in the asset conversion cycle and the company's activity (including litigation against the company) to an extent that is reasonable and possible in a summary level report

- Whether there is reasonable assurance that the financial statements are free of material mis-statements.

The auditors do not examine every financial transaction recorded in the statements; they test a certain number of transactions and generalise from these. There are Auditing Standards that lay down the fundamental principles of auditing, what constitutes audit evidence, and so on.

## Limitations of the auditing process

Auditors rely on statistical methods and usually examine only a sample of the client's financial records. If the sample is without significant error, all of the client's records are assumed to be accurate.

This statistical approach has important implications. Although auditors verify the accuracy of the company's financial statements, they do not guarantee that there are no errors in individual transactions or that there has been no fraud by management; their sampling may not detect individual errors or a well-concealed fraud. You should be aware of the limitations of an auditor's report and the importance of knowing the character of a company's management.

An audit is not a foolproof check. Several factors can undermine the accuracy and quality of an audit, including:

- The integrity of the client's management
- The integrity of the auditor
- The auditor's independence and freedom to operate
- The skill of the auditor.

If the directors try to hide something from the auditor, they have a good chance of succeeding. Similarly, if the auditor is not allowed to examine everything he or she wants, or if the auditor isn't competent, an audit may fail to reveal deficiencies in a company's accounting system and financial statements.

Since auditors are regulated professionals, they can be held legally liable for an improper audit if they have deliberately conspired with the client to overlook invalid transactions or if, because of incomplete procedures, they have failed to detect a pattern of invalid transactions. Legal liability means that those who rely on the auditor's opinion may file suit for damages if the auditor has misled them. However, auditors are not liable if they have performed a professionally competent audit and have failed to detect invalid transactions because of management deceit.

Auditors may also have civil liability for negligence if they do not exercise professional care in meeting the requirements of the contract with the client. Auditors may have third party liability, to the readers of financial statements outside the client company, if they knowingly certify any part of a statement that contains false information or inadequate disclosure of material information.

## The audit report

Upon completion of an audit, the auditor issues a report addressed to the shareholders. Contained in this report is an opinion as to whether the company's financial statements comply with GAAP and show a true and fair view.

This opinion is extremely important to lending officers because it helps them determine how much they can rely on the company's financial statements. Auditors generally give one of four opinions in an audit report:

- Unqualified
- Qualified
- Disclaimer
- Adverse.

The first two are seen most frequently. The second two are rarely seen because of their adverse effect on the audited company.

In May 1993 the introduction of *Statement of Auditing Standards: Auditors' Reports on Financial Statements* meant that all auditors began using a new standard form report that describes the responsibility of the company and of the auditor, the scope of the examination, and the opinion.

## Basic elements

Auditors' reports on financial statements should contain a clear expression of opinion, based on review and assessment of the conclusions drawn from evidence obtained in the course of the audit, and should include the following matters:

- A title identifying the person or persons to whom the report is addressed

- An introductory paragraph identifying the financial statements audited

- Separate sections, appropriately headed, dealing with:

    a)  respective responsibilities of directors (or equivalent persons) and auditors

    b)  the basis of the auditors' opinion

    c)  the auditors' opinion on the financial statements

- The manuscript or printed signature of the auditors

- The date of the auditors' report.

## Statements of responsibility

Auditors should distinguish between their responsibilities and those of the directors by including in their report:

- A statement that the financial statements are the responsibility of the reporting entity's directors (see below)

- A reference to a description of those responsibilities when set out elsewhere in the financial statements or accompanying information

- A statement that the auditors' responsibility is to express an opinion on the financial statements.

Where the financial statements or accompanying information (for example the directors' report) do not include an adequate description of directors' relevant responsibilities, the auditors' report should include a description of those responsibilities.

## Expression of opinion

Auditors should explain the basis of their opinion by including in their report:

- A statement as to their compliance or otherwise with Auditing Standards, together with the reasons for any departure

- A statement that the audit process includes:

    a) examining, on a test basis, evidence relevant to the amounts and disclosures in the financial statements

    b) assessing the significant estimates and judgements made by the reporting entity's directors in preparing the financial statements

    c) considering whether the accounting policies are appropriate to the reporting entity's circumstances, consistently applied and adequately disclosed

- A statement that they planned and performed the audit so as to obtain reasonable assurance that the financial statements are free from material mis-statement, whether caused by fraud or other irregularity or error, and that they have evaluated the overall presentation of the financial statements.

An auditor's report may include an unqualified opinion or a qualified opinion. The circumstances giving rise to each type of opinion are set out below.

## Unqualified opinion

Auditors give an unqualified opinion when the company's accounting systems are working properly. The scope of the audit provides reasonable assurance that the financial position of the company has been presented truly and fairly and in conformity with GAAP. Normally, the auditor's report is published with the financial statements when the company publishes its annual report. An unqualified opinion is the type seen most often in audited statements.

## Qualified opinion

A qualified opinion is issued when there is either a limitation on the scope of the auditors' examination or the auditors disagree with the treatment or disclosure of a matter in the financial statements, and in the auditors' judgement the effect of the matter is, or may be, material to the financial statements. Therefore those statements may not or do not give a true and fair view of the matters on which the auditors are required to report, or do not comply with relevant accounting or other requirements.

In a qualified opinion, the auditors identify the problem areas and exclude those areas from their overall opinion as to the fairness and accuracy of the company's financial statements. This exclusion is marked in the opinion letter by the words except for, unable to, do not and subject to, followed by an explanation of the items that are excluded from the opinion.

To help you through the minefield of audit reports, here is a chart that should cater for all eventualities. Note that the same points are being raised: true and fair view and materiality.

## Forming an opinion on financial statements

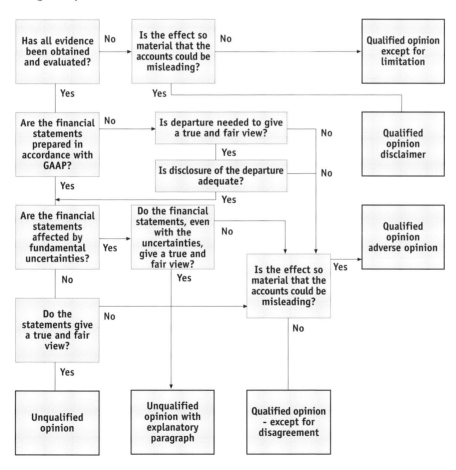

In making a qualified opinion the auditor limits his professional liability to those areas to which he has attached an unqualified opinion. A qualified opinion is a red flag; it signals that there may be significant problems with the company's financial statements and that you need to investigate thoroughly the items the auditors have excluded.

## Limitations of audit scope

When there has been a limitation on the scope of the auditors' work that prevents them from obtaining sufficient evidence to express an unqualified opinion, the auditors' report should include a description of the factors leading to the limitation in the opinion section of their report. Additionally the auditors should issue a disclaimer of opinion when the possible effect of a limitation on scope is so material or pervasive that they are unable to express an opinion on the financial statements.

A qualified opinion should be issued when the effect of the limitation is not so material or pervasive as to require a disclaimer, and the wording of the opinion should indicate that it is qualified as to the possible adjustments to the financial statements that might have been determined to be necessary had the limitation not existed.

## Disclaimer of opinion

Auditors give a disclaimer of opinion when they cannot tell whether the statements fairly represent the company's activities; they may issue a disclaimer for some of the same reasons they issue a qualified opinion, but they issue a disclaimer in cases where problems are so extensive that no opinion whatsoever can be issued. In their report, the auditors must state their reasons for issuing a disclaimer.

The disclaimer is usually marked by the words *unable to express an opinion.* By making a disclaimer of opinion, the auditor is refusing any professional responsibility for the quality of the financial statements. A disclaimer of opinion is cause for alarm. It tells you that you need to investigate thoroughly the reason for the disclaimer and determine whether you can place any reliance on the company's financial statements.

Disclaimers of opinion are rarely seen because of their adverse consequences for the audited company. The company will usually change its procedures to avoid such an opinion.

## Adverse opinion

An adverse opinion is issued when the effect of a disagreement is so material or pervasive that the auditors conclude that the financial statements are seriously misleading. An adverse opinion is expressed by stating that the financial statements do not give a true and fair view.

An adverse opinion tells you that you definitely cannot rely on the company's financial statements. Adverse opinions are relatively rare.

## Except for disagreement

When the auditors conclude that the effect of a disagreement is not so significant as to require an adverse opinion, they express an opinion that is qualified by stating that the financial statements give a true and fair view except for the effects of the matter giving rise to the disagreement.

## Fundamental uncertainty

When an inherent uncertainty exists which is fundamental, and it is adequately accounted for and disclosed in the financial statements, the auditors should include an explanatory paragraph referring to the fundamental uncertainty in the section of their report setting out the basis of their opinion. The opinion is not qualified.

## Directors' responsibilities

Company law requires the directors to prepare financial statements for each financial year which give a true and fair view of the state of affairs of the company and of the profit or loss of the company for that period. In preparing those financial statements, the directors are required to:

- Select suitable accounting policies and then apply them consistently.
- Make judgements and estimates that are reasonable and prudent.
- State whether applicable accounting standards have been followed, subject to any material departures disclosed and explained in the financial statements.
- Prepare the financial statements on the going concern basis unless it is inappropriate to presume that the company will continue in business.

The directors are responsible for keeping proper accounting records which disclose with reasonable accuracy at any time the financial position of the company and enable them to ensure that the financial statements comply with the Companies Act 1985.

They are also responsible for safeguarding the assets of the company and hence for taking reasonable steps for the prevention and detection of fraud and other irregularities.

## Unaudited financial statements

Unaudited financial statements do not carry letters of opinion regarding their fairness or compliance with GAAP. Many small companies will produce unaudited financial statements composed by either their own or an outside bookkeeper. For these companies the cost of having the statements audited by an auditor can be prohibitive and unjustifiable. In these cases you must act as 'auditor' by asking detailed questions about the composition of the statements to determine what rules were applied and what the effects of these applications are on the accounts.

Although many unaudited financial statements are prepared without an auditor's assistance, auditors do offer services in conjunction with unaudited statements: review and compilation.

# Budgeting and management accounting

# Chapter 5

# Budgeting

## Introduction

This chapter will look at the twin problem issues that businesses face internally when trying to manage themselves efficiently: budgeting and management accounting. More has been written on these two topics than just about any other business finance topic, and yet there are so few real 'rules' governing what is supposed to happen. Unlike the pure financial accounting jungle we have just journeyed through, in this internal accounting desert there are no statutory requirements and no legal requirements. We are now about to enter the world of tradition, in-breeding and error – financially speaking of course!

We will tackle the two subjects in their apparently logical order – budgeting before management accounting. What I will try to do, as is the theme of this book, is to explain certain fundamental concepts and practices and then show how you should be adopting and implementing them. What we cannot do is to say exactly how you should be doing your own budgets and satisfying your regular management information requirements; to a large extent the practice of each within your business will already be highly ritualised. For those of you who have moved jobs, you will already have seen just how different these rituals can be. Sometimes they are highly structured with tight deadlines and a massive resource requirement, yet at other times they are just quick and dirty exercises. Interestingly the performance of a business has little correlation with its ability to produce a budget, but its ability to stay in business is strongly correlated with its ability to produce adequate regular management information!

## Budgeting in general

Key Management Concept

Firstly let's look at the whole area of budgeting and the budgeting process, to see the use of a budget as a business' key planning document and also see an overview of the budgeting process. So, why exactly do we produce budgets? It is generally agreed that budgets are produced in order to plan annual activities, co-ordinate and control the business. Additionally they may well be used in a reward recognition context, as well as motivating and evaluating the performance of responsible managers. Finally they help communicate the plans of the overall business to others. In a moment we will examine in more detail each of these three topics, Control, Reward and Communication.

When producing a budget organisations typically tend to think in terms of two or hopefully all three of the following financial statements (being the three major elements of business measurement systems): profit and loss account, balance sheet and cash flow (forecast, rather than statement, in this context).

## Control

Most businesses that indulge in formalised budgeting also indulge in something that happens before that – long-term planning – so that most significant and heavyweight planning decisions will already have been taken. This long-term view then gets devolved and brought to life in the form of annual budgeting; the result of this is the production of detailed plans. Since we now have a business that has a budget, we can therefore subsequently compare actual with budgeted results, and thereby we can monitor and control business performance.

Imagine the task involved in trying to get this done within a moderately complex business. Clearly there will be massive tasks in co-ordinating and managing the various business activities that may be competing for corporate resources, reducing organisational conflict is one of the key aims at this stage. The discipline of actually sitting down, talking through and preparing a budget is deemed to be a good thing. Indeed there are some businesses that value this aspect of budgeting much more highly than what the finally produced budget figures actually say.

## Reward

Setting personal financial reward using the budgetary mechanism can often be fraught. Businesses frequently try to achieve a simple first managerial reward objective, only to find that there then follows years of haggling over definitions and the minutiae. It is very easy to introduce reward mechanisms, but very difficult to then manage them to everyone's satisfaction and expectations. Essentially the budget provides an achievable standard, and the reward/bonus/promotion mechanisms will all depend on actual performance against budget. As we will see in a later section, just as organisational structures can sometimes induce inefficiency and conflict, so can budgets.

## Communication

It is now quite clear that in order to have any chance of producing a decent budget there must be excellent understanding and co-ordination. Clear lines of communication need to be established in order to prepare the budget and then inform individuals of their particular roles within the overall scheme. As mentioned already the act of preparing a budget is often more important than the budget itself.

## Long and short-term planning

Now that we have looked briefly at the three main drivers behind why we budget, let us now review the detailed stages involved in putting a budget together. Our first point of call is to look at the relationship between the different planning horizons, long and short-term.

What is the organisation's mission and objectives, how will the strategy be translated into tactics and action?

What type of business should it be in? What are the markets and its share of those markets? What services and goods should be being sold or developed for sale? And finally, what is the required profitability and financial performance overall? Essentially this part is largely non-financial (as yet) and therefore the detail need not concern us here. But it will include such tried and tested techniques as identifying alternatives, perhaps using the marketing grid (new or existing products matching with new or existing markets) and SWOT or PEST analysis, and so on. Then the organisation needs to decide upon the optimum course of action, by matching the alternatives with the corporate objectives and mission. These then get rolled up to produce a budget (over one year) and are included into projections for several years to give a long range plan. This is a kind of bottom-up budgeting model.

An alternative way of looking at it is the top-down model whereby the long-term planning is a continuous process of monitoring, reviewing and amending – whilst budgeting is the implementation of approved programmes within the long range plan and the financial constraints. These programmes may represent any number and type of various activities from the development of new products, markets or logistics. It is the budget that translates the long range plans, programmes and financial constraints into an annual operating statement.

However, the budget is not something that originates from nothing. It is developed within the framework of a continuing business, and will largely be generated by decisions taken in previous periods as part of the longer term planning.

This philosophy that a business at any particular time is merely the sum of previously approved programmes (or projects, as we shall call them later) is an interesting and valid one. All too often we tend to think of a business as having always existed from time zero, with the same format and markets and products. However, programmes are not ballistic. Since budgets depend on

programmes, the budgeting process is not solely linked to the current year –
it is influenced by decisions in the past, present and the future.

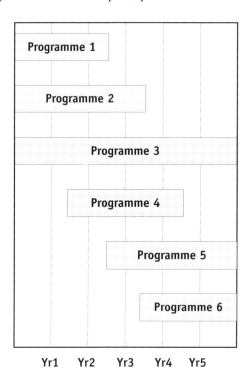

## Budget problems

We have already seen that budgets can serve several purposes; it is as well to be
aware that these purposes are likely to be in conflict in certain circumstances.
For example, budgets which are demanding may be fine for producing motivation,
but are unlikely to be accurate predictors of business results.

Equally, those designed to be of maximum benefit for planning purposes are
not likely to be of much help for performance evaluation, where actual

performance should be compared to what was strictly possible in the real circumstances, rather than what was planned as being ideal given the appropriate circumstances.

## Period for the budget

Budget periods can include all of the following, but clearly the first is going to be seen throughout all businesses: annual, quarterly, 12 monthly, for periods of 5/5/4 weeks. These last two are particularly attractive to people who find that the calendar year does not divide up particularly evenly. Some businesses actually don't even prepare annual actual financial accounts, so much do they hate the calendar year of 365 days (retailers abound here).

A variation on the theme of preparing a budget for a fixed, albeit flexible, time scale is the rolling budget. A continuous or rolling budget is where the next quarter or month budget figure is added each quarter or month. One of the advantages of rolling is that budgeting is then seen as a continuous, not discrete, process. However, a very real disadvantage is that insufficient attention is given to the future periods (quarter or month), in the belief that figures may well be changed anyway in the future.

## Budget administration

Here is a diagram that illustrates the proper structure needed to be able to budget well – something that simply doesn't happen very often. It is critically important that procedures are laid down for approval of budgets, and that support and assistance are available to budget preparers, but all procedures must be tailored appropriately to each business.

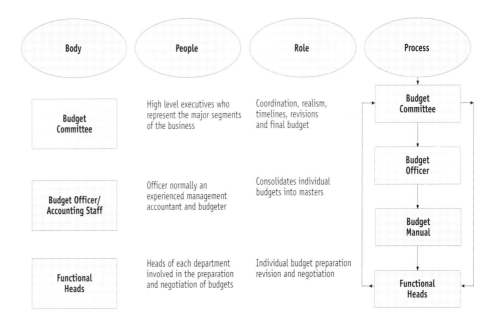

# Setting a budget

What might be the practical experience of a well-developed (in budgeting terms) business when looking at the first stage in the budgetary cycle-setting a budget? The major stages in the budgeting process are as follows.

## Critical factor

The critical factor – or what is it that restricts overall output? What will be the overall driver of volumes of activity within the organisation? We might very well like to sell a billion pounds worth of products, but if you only employ ten people it sounds an unlikely goal. Generally this critical factor will be sales, but sometimes it can be production capacity.

## Sales budget

Since generally the critical factor will be sales, the sales budget is the most important budget of all. For most profit-driven organisations the sales budget will drive the production and cost budgets, not vice-versa. Clearly this is also the most difficult to prepare, since achieving a sales budget depends on customers buying goods/services. As to how to estimate a sales budget, justifiable tactics include the opinions of experienced managers, statistical methods and market research. We will examine in more detail a little later various devices to check the validity of figures.

## Other budgets

The preparation of other budgets is normally the responsibility of the managers within those areas of activity: the bottom-up approach. This approach obtains originating information at lower levels, and refines and co-ordinates at senior levels. As to how to prepare an 'other' budget, justifiable tactics include past data and experience of the business, potential changes in future environment, and the organisation's own management and budgetary guidelines.

## Negotiation

In theory budget negotiation should move up the organisational hierarchy. Items should be agreed and consolidated at each stage, with the final version reaching the budget committee. In short, good budgeting should be a repetitive bargaining process between a budget holder and manager, and any changes should be renegotiated rather than imposed from above.

A key point to watch for is a deliberately understated budget, known as budget biasing. Equally watch out for authoritarian, imposed, unrealistic targets – the business may perhaps get short-term achievement but it's likely to be at the cost of longer term problems. The overall aim must be to achieve a meaningful budgeting process through development of trust and confidence of all parties.

## Co-ordination and review

As budgets are consolidated, there is an imperative need to check the relationship of one budget to another, their overall balance, the compatibility of constraints and plans – with a view to highlighting inconsistencies. Any problems identified need to be recycled and amended, so that finally a budgeted P&L, B/S and cash flow will be produced and even at this stage real life constraints may be identified.

## Final acceptance

When all budgets are co-ordinated and reviewed satisfactorily the master budget can then be produced. This document will be circulated, in whole or in part, to those responsible for achieving it.

*Key Learning Point*

However, a word of warning is appropriate! Budgeting is not a one-off event, as the cycle should be completed as a continuous and dynamic process. As actual results will be compared with the budget, so will monthly exception reports be generated, causes identified and corrective action taken. Sometimes causes are uncontrollable, in which case assumptions may need to be revised and the budget altered for the remainder of the period. Often the business may change its plans, this too would necessitate a change in the budget.

Many businesses nowadays change their budgets during the year, called reforecasting. This often will happen twice, or even three times a year. Each time the difference between the original budget and the reforecast (or the previous reforecast and the latest reforecast) is highlighted to show the general direction that the figures are moving in.

So far so good with the basics of why, how, who and when. But one of the most important questions asked about budgeting concerns its overall accuracy. We all know that budgets cannot be accurate, but how can we get them to be as accurate as possible?

## Reviewing a budget

### Inherent uncertainty

Budgeting involves predicting the future. Since the future is unpredictable, it follows that budgets are inherently uncertain and inaccurate. Whenever there is uncertainty about the future it is advisable to assess the extent of the uncertainty and the effect it will have on budgets, especially in respect of unforeseen events, critical items and risk.

At the end of the day, what a Finance Director wants most of all is a budget that is going to be 100% accurate, in other words, no surprises please! What they don't want is a budget that they are told is achievable, but which is then significantly under (or even over) achieved. Remember, no surprises, and so what the FD wants is a set of tools that will test the 'last year plus 10%' type of budgets that abound everywhere. The FD simply has absolutely no idea, when you submit a single figure (last year's plus 10%), whether that figure is achievable, how achievable it is, what is the range of possible outcomes, what is the risk, and so on. So much for the single figure approach, and yet it is what most of us rely on!

There are some generally accepted methods of analysing uncertainty, of which the most important probably are three-level budgets, probability analysis, sensitivity analysis, and zero-based (or bottom-up) budgeting.

## Three level budgets

This is one of the most fundamental forms of analysis, and dispenses with probabilities altogether. Essentially three outcomes (known in the trade as 'states of the world') are required to be prepared on the basis of each manager's estimate of the most likely, worst possible and best possible outcomes. All the figures should be rationally and logically produced, with the worst and best possible outcomes being based on realistic assumptions. By estimating these outcomes the budget committee is aware of the range of possible outcomes in results which may be produced by the current budget.

At last the FD has something else apart from the single figure budget. However, he still has little idea as to how 'confident' the budgeter is about achieving the best/most likely/worst case outcomes.

Take an example of a business which had sales of £10m last year. The 'last year plus 10%' school of thinking would probably submit a budget of £11m. Using the three level approach the sales director estimates that in a good year he could hit £15m, but a bad year would probably show more like £8m. This is, of course, very informative to the FD who now has a slightly better feel for the situation. However, he has a problem when he comes to add up all the individual budgets. Does he take the best from everyone, or does he use his judgement to select some 'best', some 'most likely' and some 'worst'; if so, which ones? Back to square one, perhaps!

## Probability analysis

The last described problem can be partially solved by probability analysis. This can be used at varying levels of complexity, always bearing in mind that what we are attempting to do is measure the uncertain. Techniques such as decision tree or probability analysis places probabilities against events and computes an expected value for overall profit. A standard deviation of the expected value may be calculated, indicating a measure of risk in the budget. Management may then select the appropriate budget with regard to their own perspective on risk and return.

The probabilities for each of the following variables may be assessed, and a probabilistic budget built up containing such things as: sales volume, sales mix of products sold, unit variable costs, fixed costs, probability of strikes, wage inflation, new product launch and timing, new systems and so on.

To use our example, we have already estimated the states as being:

| State | Result £m |
|---|---|
| Best | 15 |
| Most likely | 11 |
| Worst | 8 |

The sales director says that he thinks the probability of each state happening is 70% for the most likely, 20% for the best and 10% for the worst. We can then insert the figures alongside the others in the table, and then multiply the two columns. Adding the products gives us our result.

| State | Result £m | Probability | Product £m |
|---|---|---|---|
| Best | 15 | 20% | 3.0 |
| Most likely | 11 | 70% | 7.7 |
| Worst | 8 | 10% | 0.8 |
| | | 100% | 11.5 |

The expected value obtained is £11.5m, a figure that we are likely to put greater reliance on. Again this gives the FD extremely valuable information. This technique of multiplying potential outcomes by their respective probability and then adding the results together is known as an 'expected value', or EV.

Simply putting a lot of thought into the process, advocates say, ensures that the result is a more than credible alternative to the single figure option. One of the strictly mathematical ripostes to EV is that EV is the average result of an infinitely large number of trials – yet in real life there is only one event. This means that in real life we will get either £8m or £11m or £15m, but nothing in between. But that's all getting a bit theoretical!

## Sensitivity analysis

Sensitivity analysis has been with us for many years and tests the responsiveness of profitability, cash flow and budgetary figures to changes in one or more of the underlying assumptions, for example:

- An unforeseen 10% rise in production cost due to material price increases
- A shortfall of 10% in sales volume owing to inefficient market
- A decrease of 10% in selling price due to increased competition
- An increase in fixed overheads of 10% following rates increase.

Whilst sensitivity analysis provides 'what if' information, it doesn't give answers to the likelihood of a situation occurring. Certain spreadsheets now have a built-in 'scenario modeller' which facilitates the interrogation and production of scenario analysis.

Whilst all of the techniques above will help to winkle out the 'last year plus' recidivists, the real professional tool to do this is in fact the next one: zero-based budgeting.

# Zero-based budgeting

## Purpose of zero-based budgeting (ZBB)

One of the most significant drawbacks of traditional budgeting is the inability to 'get behind' the persistent last year plus approach. A more polite way of saying that is the phrase incremental budgeting. Whilst this may be acceptable for many items, the problem is that any historic errors are likely to be continued. Put simply, the FD doesn't know why Marketing needs twelve people – why not ten instead? Just because they had twelve last year doesn't mean that number were really needed at all. But how does the FD solve this, and challenge the figures more strongly?

The answer is that he turns to ZBB. Any of you who have lived through a ZBB exercise will not have forgotten it in a hurry. Those of you who are not sure whether you have experienced it are quite likely to have gone though it, it's just that your management decided to call it anything rather than ZBB, those words themselves tend to strike fear into the listener. ZBB has become a feared concept but much of what it does is actually beneficial. Some liken it to the sound of folk digging their own graves, some to the sound of the organisation gaining financial enlightenment, it depends where you sit. ZBB also happens to fit nicely with the modern management practice of team and project working, rather than the traditional blinkered departmental model, as we will see later. If you haven't already done it, perhaps you should think about it. But, a word of warning: try to be realistic about what you are doing, and read the chapter in this book on relevant costs for decision making first!

The most important point about ZBB is that you probably won't be using it in areas that themselves have other adequate measurement methods. Instead you will use it on those traditional 'bar of soap' areas, where you simply have no idea what the right figure should be. These tend to be those areas not already tightly controlled, typically non-manufacturing, discretionary or support areas. Candidates can include sales, marketing, finance, administration, IT, facilities management and so on. As you can guess, the trendy alternative to doing things such as these yourself is to outsource it.

## The principle of ZBB

The principle of ZBB is that the preparation of the master budget should build on individual budgets, as before, but the content of those individual budgets will now be different. Each budget starts from scratch, or zero, as if the budget were being prepared for the first time. Every cost and item of expenditure has to be justified. In practice one often works downwards to see what would happen if expenditure is cut back. Whatever, the principle of ZBB is that it challenges and provides a cost-benefit for every item. It asks questions such as: should this function be performed at all? What should the activity level be? How much should we do? Is this the right/only way of doing this? How much should this activity cost?

Firstly managers specify 'decision packages' for their area of the business. These packages are like building blocks of activities. Each block must have a cost associated with it and a service level that the business will enjoy. At last you can get your hands on that elusive bar of soap! The only golden rule here is that the fundamental package must not be the same as guess what? Last year plus 10%, of course! Secondly, all packages are subjected to senior management evaluation, and are ranked according to what they subjectively consider to be most important to the business as a whole. Once available resources are allocated according to the ranking, anything not included will be cast adrift. Quite a harsh regime, but quite a useful one if these type of costs have always proved elusive to you and your organisation.

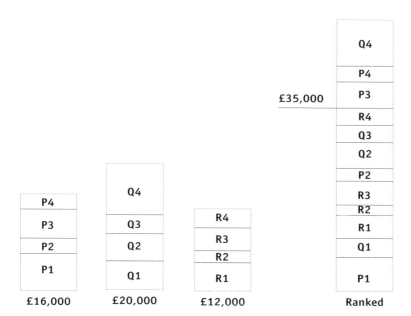

## Advantages of ZBB

Traditional budgeting tends simply to extrapolate existing accepted levels of activity and cost. The status quo is preserved and cost relationships are not challenged, whereas ZBB allocates resources by need and benefit. It encourages a questioning approach to existing costs and long standing assumptions. It concentrates on the relationship between outputs (not inputs) and value for money. In theory, it leads to greater staff involvement, motivation and interest. Whereas, in traditional budgeting alternatives are often ignored, they are considered in ZBB. It encourages working in cross-functional teams and an understanding of the whole business.

## Disadvantages of ZBB

It is a massively time-consuming exercise, as suddenly people have to discover financial information about themselves that they previously simply weren't aware of. In light of this you should consider rotating or selecting to whom it will apply each year. It may well over emphasise short-term benefits at the expense of the long-term. It promotes the misconception that all decision-making takes place in the budgeting process, and not thereafter. It requires a high level of subjectivity at the management level for ranking. Behaviourally it can be very difficult to introduce, owing to the reasons already described.

Surveys show that in many cases ZBB has lead to significant improvements, and any lack of success is largely due to a lack of management support, combined with difficulty in quantifying relevant output measures to quantify that success.

## Budgeting behaviour in organisations

We have examined control from the point of view of variances, but the effect on people is less emphasised. The problems are that 'playing' the game becomes more important than the result, delegation and decentralisation increase any existing fragmented loyalties.

## Motivation

Motivation is driven by many issues, but the results of poor motivation could just as well include any of the following excuses. How many of them sound familiar?

- I'm too busy to participate in budgets, I've got too much to do; besides, budgets are low priority

- A formal budget is constricting – there is no flexibility for my operation

- Since there is slack built in to the budget, I'm not too bothered if I don't make my targets

- I don't really care what the rest of the business is doing

- I'll put in just enough effort to achieve the plan

- Since it's in the budget, I'll spend up to the limit; I have no incentive to save

- It's just a way for management to exert pressure.

## Your business

*Activity*

You might just like to reflect on your own business sometime in the near future, and use this little checklist as a prompt for your thoughts. As far as your own organisation is concerned, consider the attitude/policy towards the following items:

- What is the management style: democracy or hierarchy?

- Is there much conflict of personal and corporate aspirations?

- Is there deliberate slack in the budget?

- How does the organisation ensure that budgets are attained?

## Cash budgeting

Before we move on to monitoring a budget and tracking actual against expected performance, we need to resurrect the idea that simply concentrating on the profit and loss account is insufficient.

Take, for example, a business with different departments – all of whom are preparing budgets. As a finance director I receive all the profit and loss account budgets, which promise excellent growth. So far, so good.

Tragically though, when I come to add all these individually virtuous budgets to get the organisational whole, I find that the business does not have access to sufficient cash resources to undertake the activities.

A critical part of the budgeting process, therefore, is the preparation of the cash flow forecast.

On the following pages there are three cash flow forecasts. All are identical except for the assumptions about the timing of cash flows from sales receipts. Let's start by running through the first one; after that the second and third should be straightforward enough, but stunning in their message.

| Profit & Loss | Annual | Month | % | Timing | Jul | Aug | Sep | Oct | Nov | Dec | Jan | Feb | Mar | Apr | May | Jun | TOTAL |
|---|---|---|---|---|---|---|---|---|---|---|---|---|---|---|---|---|---|
| Sales | 1920 | 160 | 100 | 100% cash | 160 | 160 | 160 | 160 | 160 | 160 | 160 | 160 | 160 | 160 | 160 | 160 | 1,920 |
| | | | | **Receipts** | 160 | 160 | 160 | 160 | 160 | 160 | 160 | 160 | 160 | 160 | 160 | 160 | 1,920 |
| Purchases | 240 | 20 | 13 | 1 mth arr | 0 | 20 | 20 | 20 | 20 | 20 | 20 | 20 | 20 | 20 | 20 | 20 | 220 |
| Direct labour | 576 | 48 | 30 | immediate | 48 | 48 | 48 | 48 | 48 | 48 | 48 | 48 | 48 | 48 | 48 | 48 | 576 |
| Transport | 144 | 12 | 8 | immediate | 12 | 12 | 12 | 12 | 12 | 12 | 12 | 12 | 12 | 12 | 12 | 12 | 144 |
| sub-total | 960 | 80 | 50 | | | | | | | | | | | | | | |
| Gross profit | 960 | 80 | 50 | | | | | | | | | | | | | | |
| Rent | 48 | 4 | 3 | 1 mth adv | 8 | 4 | 4 | 4 | 4 | 4 | 4 | 4 | 4 | 4 | 4 | 4 | 52 |
| Heat light power | 12 | 1 | 1 | 1 mth arr | 0 | 1 | 1 | 1 | 1 | 1 | 1 | 1 | 1 | 1 | 1 | 1 | 11 |
| Insurance | 12 | 1 | 1 | 6 mths adv | 6 | 0 | 0 | 0 | 0 | 0 | 6 | 0 | 0 | 0 | 0 | 0 | 12 |
| Advertising | 96 | 8 | 5 | 1 mth arr | 0 | 8 | 8 | 8 | 8 | 8 | 8 | 8 | 8 | 8 | 8 | 8 | 88 |
| Interest | 48 | 4 | 3 | 1 mth arr | 0 | 4 | 4 | 4 | 4 | 4 | 4 | 4 | 4 | 4 | 4 | 4 | 44 |
| Sals - directors | 192 | 16 | 10 | immediate | 16 | 16 | 16 | 16 | 16 | 16 | 16 | 16 | 16 | 16 | 16 | 16 | 192 |
| Sals - others | 72 | 6 | 4 | immediate | 6 | 6 | 6 | 6 | 6 | 6 | 6 | 6 | 6 | 6 | 6 | 6 | 72 |
| Royalties @ 10% | 192 | 16 | 10 | 1 mth arr | 0 | 16 | 16 | 16 | 16 | 16 | 16 | 16 | 16 | 16 | 16 | 16 | 176 |
| sub-total | 672 | 56 | 35 | **Payments** | 96 | 135 | 135 | 135 | 135 | 135 | 141 | 135 | 135 | 135 | 135 | 135 | 1,587 |
| Net profit | 288 | 24 | 15 | **Month flow** | 64 | 25 | 25 | 25 | 25 | 25 | 19 | 25 | 25 | 25 | 25 | 25 | 333 |
| | | | | **Cumulative** | 64 | 89 | 114 | 139 | 164 | 189 | 208 | 233 | 258 | 283 | 308 | 333 | |

| Balance Sheet | |
|---|---|
| Current Assets | |
| Sales | 0 |
| Rent prepaid | 4 |
| Cash | 333 |
| Sub-total | 337 |
| Current Liabilities | |
| Purchases | 20 |
| Heat light | 1 |
| Advert | 8 |
| Interest | 4 |
| Royalties | 16 |
| Sub-total | 49 |
| Total | 288 |

The four columns on the left make up a projected Profit and Loss. This is a list of sales, cost of sales and other costs. The first and last key-lined columns give all this information, and also show a month and percentage column. The second key-lined column gives the assumptions about the timings of receipts and payments: advance, arrears, immediate, and how many months.

The cash columns (next 13 columns) simply pick up the amount of the monthly cash flow and put it in the appropriate month. In this first example we are strongly cash generative, mainly because we assume that all the cash arises in the first month of activity – not very realistic.

The point to illustrate here is one of the relationship between cash flow, profit and loss and balance sheet. Look to see how the spreadsheet generates the balance sheet in the columns on the right. It does so by comparing the profit and loss account figure with the total cash figure.

Look at the profit and loss account figure for sales (£1,920) and compare it with the total cash figure from sales (£1,920). There is no difference, and therefore the figure in the balance sheet shown as current assets sales will be nil.

Now look at the profit and loss account figure for purchases (£240) and compare it with the total cash figure for purchases (£220). There is a difference of £20, which relates to one month's worth of purchases. This will be shown in current liabilities as purchases.

The process is repeated for all items, and the balance sheet generated from this should not surprise you with its total, £288, or the amount of the originally projected profit.

Now this is all very straightforward, but critically important when dwelling on the subject of cash budgeting. Let us now change just one figure, the way in which we collect cash from sales, and see its effect on our funding requirements.

| Profit & Loss | Annual | Month | % |
|---|---|---|---|
| Sales | 1920 | 160 | 100 |
| Purchases | 240 | 20 | 13 |
| Direct labour | 576 | 48 | 30 |
| Transport | 144 | 12 | 8 |
| sub-total | 960 | 80 | 50 |
| Gross profit | 960 | 80 | 50 |
| Rent | 48 | 4 | 3 |
| Heat light power | 12 | 1 | 1 |
| Insurance | 12 | 1 | 1 |
| Advertising | 96 | 8 | 5 |
| Interest | 48 | 4 | 3 |
| Sals - directors | 192 | 16 | 10 |
| Sals - others | 72 | 6 | 4 |
| Royalties @ 10% | 192 | 16 | 10 |
| sub-total | 672 | 56 | 35 |
| Net profit | 288 | 24 | 15 |

| Timing | Jul | Aug | Sep | Oct | Nov | Dec | Jan | Feb | Mar | Apr | May | Jun | TOTAL |
|---|---|---|---|---|---|---|---|---|---|---|---|---|---|
| 50% cash | 80 | 80 | 80 | 80 | 80 | 80 | 80 | 80 | 80 | 80 | 80 | 80 | 960 |
| 50% +2 mth | 0 | 0 | 80 | 80 | 80 | 80 | 80 | 80 | 80 | 80 | 80 | 80 | 800 |
| Receipts | 80 | 80 | 160 | 160 | 160 | 160 | 160 | 160 | 160 | 160 | 160 | 160 | 1,760 |
| 1 mth arr | 0 | 20 | 20 | 20 | 20 | 20 | 20 | 20 | 20 | 20 | 20 | 20 | 220 |
| immediate | 48 | 48 | 48 | 48 | 48 | 48 | 48 | 48 | 48 | 48 | 48 | 48 | 576 |
| immediate | 12 | 12 | 12 | 12 | 12 | 12 | 12 | 12 | 12 | 12 | 12 | 12 | 144 |
| 1 mth adv | 8 | 4 | 4 | 4 | 4 | 4 | 4 | 4 | 4 | 4 | 4 | 4 | 52 |
| 1 mth arr | 0 | 1 | 1 | 1 | 1 | 1 | 1 | 1 | 1 | 1 | 1 | 1 | 11 |
| 6 mths adv | 6 | 0 | 0 | 0 | 0 | 0 | 6 | 0 | 0 | 0 | 0 | 0 | 12 |
| 1 mth arr | 0 | 8 | 8 | 8 | 8 | 8 | 8 | 8 | 8 | 8 | 8 | 8 | 88 |
| 1 mth arr | 0 | 4 | 4 | 4 | 4 | 4 | 4 | 4 | 4 | 4 | 4 | 4 | 44 |
| immediate | 16 | 16 | 16 | 16 | 16 | 16 | 16 | 16 | 16 | 16 | 16 | 16 | 192 |
| immediate | 6 | 6 | 6 | 6 | 6 | 6 | 6 | 6 | 6 | 6 | 6 | 6 | 72 |
| 1 mth arr | 0 | 16 | 16 | 16 | 16 | 16 | 16 | 16 | 16 | 16 | 16 | 16 | 176 |
| Payments | 96 | 135 | 135 | 135 | 135 | 135 | 141 | 135 | 135 | 135 | 135 | 135 | 1,587 |
| Month flow | -16 | -55 | 25 | 25 | 25 | 25 | 19 | 25 | 25 | 25 | 25 | 25 | 173 |
| Cumulative | -16 | -71 | -46 | -21 | 4 | 29 | 48 | 73 | 98 | 123 | 148 | 173 | |

| Balance Sheet | |
|---|---|
| Current Assets | |
| Sales | 160 |
| Rent prepaid | 4 |
| Cash | 173 |
| Sub-total | 337 |
| Current Liabilities | |
| Creditors | 20 |
| Heat light | 1 |
| Advert | 8 |
| Interest | 4 |
| Royalties | 16 |
| Sub-total | 49 |
| Total | 288 |

All expense figures are the same, so all we have done is to swap £160 of cash from the previous example into debtors. Same profit, same everything, but we now know we would have to be talking to the bank in advance to get their agreement to an overdraft. The amount of this overdraft we can see should be around £71 (the maximum in-year overdrawn balance). Quite a difference from the first example!

Finally, let's change the sales assumption still further (3 months), and see what the picture is – quite shocking, isn't it? The moral of the story is make sure you do cash budgeting.

| Profit & Loss | Annual | Month | % | Timing | Jul | Aug | Sep | Oct | Nov | Dec | Jan | Feb | Mar | Apr | May | Jun | TOTAL | Balance Sheet | |
|---|---|---|---|---|---|---|---|---|---|---|---|---|---|---|---|---|---|---|---|
| Sales | 1920 | 160 | 100 | | | | | | | | | | | | | | | Current Assets | |
| | | | | 100% +3 mth | 0 | 0 | 0 | 160 | 160 | 160 | 160 | 160 | 160 | 160 | 160 | 160 | 1,440 | Sales | 480 |
| | | | | Receipts | 0 | 0 | 0 | 160 | 160 | 160 | 160 | 160 | 160 | 160 | 160 | 160 | 1,440 | Rent prepaid | 4 |
| Purchases | 240 | 20 | 13 | 1 mth arr | 0 | 20 | 20 | 20 | 20 | 20 | 20 | 20 | 20 | 20 | 20 | 20 | 220 | Cash | -147 |
| Direct labour | 576 | 48 | 30 | immediate | 48 | 48 | 48 | 48 | 48 | 48 | 48 | 48 | 48 | 48 | 48 | 48 | 576 | Sub-tot | 337 |
| Transport | 144 | 12 | 8 | immediate | 12 | 12 | 12 | 12 | 12 | 12 | 12 | 12 | 12 | 12 | 12 | 12 | 144 | | |
| sub-total | 960 | 80 | 50 | | | | | | | | | | | | | | | Current Liabilities | |
| Gross profit | 960 | 80 | 50 | | | | | | | | | | | | | | | Creditors | 20 |
| | | | | | | | | | | | | | | | | | | Heat light | 1 |
| Rent | 48 | 4 | 3 | 1 mth adv | 8 | 4 | 4 | 4 | 4 | 4 | 4 | 4 | 4 | 4 | 4 | 4 | 52 | Advert | 8 |
| Heat light power | 12 | 1 | 1 | 1 mth arr | 0 | 1 | 1 | 1 | 1 | 1 | 1 | 1 | 1 | 1 | 1 | 1 | 11 | Interest | 4 |
| Insurance | 12 | 1 | 1 | 6 mths adv | 6 | 0 | 0 | 0 | 0 | 0 | 6 | 0 | 0 | 0 | 0 | 0 | 12 | Royalties | 16 |
| Advertising | 96 | 8 | 5 | 1 mth arr | 0 | 8 | 8 | 8 | 8 | 8 | 8 | 8 | 8 | 8 | 8 | 8 | 88 | Sub-tot | 49 |
| Interest | 48 | 4 | 3 | 1 mth arr | 0 | 4 | 4 | 4 | 4 | 4 | 4 | 4 | 4 | 4 | 4 | 4 | 44 | | |
| Sals - directors | 192 | 16 | 10 | immediate | 16 | 16 | 16 | 16 | 16 | 16 | 16 | 16 | 16 | 16 | 16 | 16 | 192 | Total | 288 |
| Sals - others | 72 | 6 | 4 | immediate | 6 | 6 | 6 | 6 | 6 | 6 | 6 | 6 | 6 | 6 | 6 | 6 | 72 | | |
| Royalties @ 10% | 192 | 16 | 10 | 1 mth arr | 0 | 16 | 16 | 16 | 16 | 16 | 16 | 16 | 16 | 16 | 16 | 16 | 176 | | |
| sub-total | 672 | 56 | 35 | Payments | 96 | 135 | 135 | 135 | 135 | 135 | 141 | 135 | 135 | 135 | 135 | 135 | 1,587 | | |
| Net profit | 288 | 24 | 15 | Month flow | -96 | -135 | -135 | 25 | 25 | 25 | 19 | 25 | 25 | 25 | 25 | 25 | -147 | | |
| | | | | Cumulative | -96 | -231 | -366 | -341 | -316 | -291 | -272 | -247 | -222 | -197 | -172 | -147 | | | |

By the way, don't go around thinking that these spreadsheets are models of excellence. They are missing several things, which you might like to think about:

- Initial capital spend
- Sales start at 100% of projections
- No VAT taken into account
- No taxation
- No real interest calculation
- No start-up effect.

# Monitoring a budget

## Definition and purposes of budgetary control

*'Budgetary control is the establishment of budgets relating the responsibilities of managers to the requirements of policy, together with the continuous comparison of actual and budgeted results – either to achieve that aim or to revise it.'*

Therefore, it should include clear and succinct guidelines dealing with the following:

- Targets for the organisation or department, and what happens if targets are not met

- How to identify and explain differences in actual performance, and suggest corrective action

- When and how a plan should be revised

- Establishment of standard costs

- Employee performance criteria.

Budgetary control is part of the control cycle, and is an interactive process of planning, monitoring and control. Feedback is the modification or control of a process or system by its results or effects, using the differences between planned and actual results (feedback loop).

Historical costs are always used in budgetary control, since the current period results are derived from events that have already happened and cannot therefore be changed. A budgetary control system uses past events as a means of controlling/adjusting future planned activities.

## Budget realism

Although control theory is common sense and correct, there are practical problems with the assumptions involved:

- The initial budget has to be realistic in content and acceptable to those who have to implement it

- Are the actual results produced by the information systems actually accurate?

- Is feedback sufficiently timely (is it produced on time) to enable corrective action to be taken?

- What are the causes of the differences?

- Has everyone in the organisation been kept informed?

- Is the initial plan realistic – if it isn't then what is the point of analysing variances?

## Control limits

There are certain generally accepted guidelines for exception reporting. For example, certain items must always be reviewed, such as profit centre profitability, total costs and so on. Also certain control items tend to be pre-determined, such as how large does the difference have to be before it is investigated and corrective action taken? Exceptional variances will probably be highlighted, focusing attention on those items where performance differs significantly from standard or budget.

## Comparing actual and budget

Simply examining the mathematical differences between budgeted and actual results will provide the fundamental information concerning performance, but how sophisticated is this? A better way to compare actual and budget is to use a flexible budget.

A flexible budget is one where, by recognising the differences in behaviour between fixed and variable costs in relation to fluctuating levels in output, turnover or other variable factors such as number of employees, it changes appropriately with fluctuations! Many costs are fixed, depreciation, rent and wages, and the increase in the number of service industries generally means that direct costs are proportionately smaller. The flexible budget helps tell apart differences from volume and those from excessive unit costs or lower sales price.

## Marginal or total costing

A debate can now arise over which costing method to use, marginal or total absorbtion costing. The choice depends to a large extent on the system already in operation in the business. As for the differences between full and marginal costing, here is a reminder of the advantages and disadvantages of each.

Full costing shows the total cost of the product and thereby product profitability (to be discussed in a later section). But it is sometimes difficult to understand, is often complicated and time consuming to prepare, and is of course highly subjective.

Marginal costing on the other hand is easier to understand, and it makes budgeting and variance analysis very much simpler. However it has some significant disadvantages. It can over-emphasise short-term results, and because it can possibly confuse contribution with profit it may encourage selling at below true cost.

As far as other matters are concerned, there should always be comparison of actual for one period to actual for the previous period, and actual for one period to budget for that period.

# Management accounting

*Key Management Concept*

## Responsibility and variances – an improvement on the common-sense approach

The common-sense approach is that a variance means what it says, the difference between two figures. However the traditional model of variance analysis and reporting does not always provide this information; for example the budget may be out of date, or simply unrealistic.

We have already looked at the desirability of comparing actual results to a flexed or flexible budget, in order to eliminate the volume or capacity differences between planned and actual production. That is one improvement.

Another improvement is as follows. Variances should be reported by taking as the main starting point not the original budget or standard but a budget or standard which can be seen, with hindsight, to be the best that could have been achieved. Hindsight is such a wonderful thing, but really in this case altering the original expectation is of course entirely sensible. Take an example where the sales volume is significantly hit by unforeseen circumstances. Production will obviously reduce accordingly. But, unless the new changed way of reporting is adopted, variance analysis within production will throw up excellent positive variances. Savings on materials, labour and so on all rather miss the point, production wasn't efficient, it was non-existent!

# A more realistic standard

This approach suggests that a business should compare actual results with what it deems it should have accomplished. This is a type of 'opportunity cost' approach. The definitions used include the following words. *Ex ante* refers to the original budget or standard, whereas *ex post* refers to the original budget or standard that should perhaps have been in place (with hindsight) as more appropriate.

The opportunity cost approach is based on the principle that variances ought to give a realistic value as to what they have cost the organisation; in other words the profit lost or gained as a result of that decision or difference.

Variances which are due to differences between the *ex ante* and *ex post* have nothing to do with operating results, they are differences due to planning items alone.

This is an interesting variation to the theme of traditional variance analysis, which implies that actual real-life performance is always at fault and nothing else is. The addition of planning variances to the existing operating variances provide another dimension to variance analysis, as can be seen below.

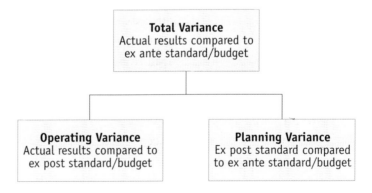

## Planning and operational variances

A planning variance will be adverse when the ex post standard is more pessimistic than the original *ex ante* standard. A similar but opposite situation applies whereby a planning variance will be favourable when the *ex post* standard is more optimistic than the original *ex ante* standard. Planning variances can reveal a severe weakness in budgeting procedures which, for the sake of the business's health, must be rectified for future periods. Further analysis can be made to split between possibly avoidable and unavoidable planning errors. The former give rise to lost profits, but the latter result in poor quality budgets which may not have altered profit expectations.

However, we must also recognise that there are limitations in using planning and operational variances, the most important is just what should a more realistic standard have been? In analysing the unavoidable and possibly avoidable planning variances there has to be a very close replacement/substitute for the originally planned item, otherwise it just doesn't make sense.

## Reasons for variances occurring

The excessive or favourable cost may be controllable, or it may be uncontrollable. If it is controllable, then is it so by the direct manager, or is it controllable by someone else? Is it controllable by anyone at all, or is it simply beyond the control of anyone in the business? Are the standards inaccurate, due to poor quality or deliberately optimistic figures included primarily for the purpose of incentivisation? Also, always remember that one adverse may be cancelled out by one favourable variance; a calm exterior may conceal a chaotic organisation beneath.

## Controllable and uncontrollable costs

Most variable costs are deemed to be controllable, even though a manager may not be able to influence the purchase price of a material, say. Transfer pricing and recharge of internal costs is not a valid debate. Although fixed costs are generally seen as uncontrollable costs, some may not be. Directly attributable fixed costs may be avoided/reduced, albeit by drastic methods of control. Retained authority by head office includes certain key costs.

## When to investigate variances

Generally we tend to use cost-benefit analysis to determine whether the cost of investigating and following up a variance is actually going to be worthwhile. If variances are highly interdependent then an analysis may not be efficient. We typically express the variance as a percentage of, say, standard or budgeted cost – and we use this as a measure for materiality. We also need to make allowances for an element of 'expected' or normal adverse variances; statistically this must happen, as life itself has its random ups and downs. Finally, do take a longer view of variances; on a cumulative basis any variance shown now may simply change or disappear. Trying to fit results into artificial monthly or quarterly periods is always likely to be fundamentally distorting.

If only businesses provided some elementary training in the whole budget procedure then, having participated in the standard setting, managers would be more willing to accept responsibility for what happened thereafter. Provided that the standards are seen to be reasonable, participation is likely to be increased. Finally, the regular variance reports must be produced on a timely basis and distributed to all concerned, and the reports should include both current period and cumulative to date.

A typical analysis of variances would look like this:

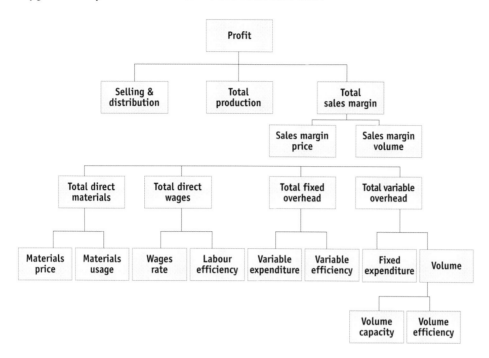

## Better management accounting

Although this comes at the end of this chapter, it really is the most important part of it. In a later chapter we look at all things from product profitability to pricing, in general trying to take a more enlightened view as to how well the company is performing.

The problem is that your accountant will nearly always feel happier giving you a traditional profit and loss account. However the traditional profit and loss account 'dump' almost always gives you absolutely no really useful information to help manage your business into the future.

You could think of it like a trade-off, or a continuum. The more useful management information is to you at the coalface, the less it is useful to an accountant, and vice versa. What tends to happen is that mediocrity prevails and no one wins.

I am deeply shocked by the generally appalling level of management information that large and seemingly successful companies prepare for internal consumption. Equally, I am constantly amazed at some smaller businesses who have the problem licked into shape.

What I would desperately encourage you to do is to start pressurising your accountants to provide you with decent and useful information. To show you what some people achieve, here are some examples.

| | CURRENT MONTH | | | | | | YEAR TO DATE | | | | | |
|---|---|---|---|---|---|---|---|---|---|---|---|---|
| | ACTUAL | | PLAN | | LAST YEAR | | ACTUAL | | PLAN | | LAST YEAR | |
| SALES (External) | £ | GP% | £ | GP% | £ | GP% | £ | GP% | £ | GP% | £ | GP% |
| TIMBER | 36 | 31.8 | 42 | 30.0 | 34 | 30.5 | 129 | 30.6 | 160 | 30.0 | 127 | 27.9 |
| SHEET MATERIALS | 15 | 22.7 | 16 | 25.5 | 14 | 22.8 | 52 | 23.6 | 63 | 25.5 | 61 | 25.5 |
| JOINERY | 24 | 19.1 | 15 | 22.0 | 11 | 21.1 | 70 | 19.6 | 56 | 22.0 | 47 | 20.3 |
| MATERIALS | 137 | 30.3 | 133 | 32.2 | 131 | 35.7 | 495 | 28.7 | 510 | 32.2 | 468 | 34.6 |
| FITTINGS | 19 | 31.6 | 23 | 26.0 | 22 | 25.1 | 89 | 27.8 | 88 | 26.0 | 78 | 23.9 |
| BRANCH SALES | 231 | 29.1 | 229 | 30.0 | 213 | 32.1 | 835 | 27.8 | 876 | 30.0 | 780 | 30.9 |
| OTHER SALES | 205 | 8.7 | 188 | 9.0 | 190 | 7.4 | 695 | 7.9 | 720 | 9.0 | 713 | 7.4 |
| TOTAL SALES | 436 | 19.3 | 417 | 20.5 | 403 | 20.5 | 1530 | 18.7 | 1596 | 20.5 | 1493 | 19.7 |
| | | | | | | | | | | | | |
| CASH SALES | 58 | | 41 | | 46 | | 158 | | 158 | | 140 | |
| CREDIT SALES | 378 | | 375 | | 357 | | 1372 | | 1439 | | 1353 | |
| | | | | | | | | | | | | |
| DELIVERED SALES | 121 | | 116 | | 108 | | 437 | | 447 | | 395 | |
| | | | | | | | | | | | | |
| ACTIVE CUSTOMERS | 340 | | | | 330 | | 320 | | | | 320 | |

| ANALYSIS | JAN | FEB | MAR | APR | MAY | JUN | JUL | AUG | SEP | OCT | NOV | DEC | AVG |
|---|---|---|---|---|---|---|---|---|---|---|---|---|---|
| SALES PER DAY THIS Yr. | | | | | | | | | | | | | |
| BRANCH SALES | 8 | 9 | 11 | 12 | | | | | | | | | 10 |
| OTHER SALES | 7 | 7 | 9 | 11 | | | | | | | | | 8 |
| SALES PER DAY LAST Yr. | | | | | | | | | | | | | |
| BRANCH SALES | 8 | 9 | 10 | 11 | | | | | | | | | 9 |
| OTHER SALES | 7 | 10 | 9 | 9 | | | | | | | | | 9 |

| | ACTUAL | | PLAN | | LAST YEAR | | ACTUAL | | PLAN | | LAST YEAR | |
|---|---|---|---|---|---|---|---|---|---|---|---|---|
| PROFITABILITY | | | | | | | | | | | | |
| GR.PROFIT BRANCH | 67 | 29.1 | 69 | 30.0 | 69 | 32.1 | 232 | 27.8 | 263 | 30.0 | 241 | 30.9 |
| GR.PROFIT OTHER | 18 | 8.7 | 17 | 9.0 | 14 | 7.4 | 55 | 7.9 | 65 | 9.0 | 53 | 7.4 |
| TOTAL GR.PROFIT | 85 | 19.5 | 86 | 20.5 | 83 | 20.5 | 287 | 18.8 | 328 | 20.5 | 294 | 19.7 |
| | | | | | | | | | | | | |
| STAFF COSTS | -24 | 5.5 | -22 | 5.0 | -22 | 5.0 | -86 | 19.7 | -87 | 20.0 | -83 | 19.0 |
| OTHER COSTS | -18 | 4.1 | -17 | 3.9 | -19 | 4.4 | -71 | 16.3 | -67 | 15.4 | -76 | 17.4 |
| BAD DEBTS | -2 | 0.5 | -2 | 0.5 | -1 | 0.2 | -21 | 4.8 | -9 | 2.1 | -5 | 1.1 |
| RENT | -3 | 0.7 | -3 | 0.7 | -3 | 0.7 | -12 | 2.8 | -12 | 2.8 | -12 | 2.8 |
| BRANCH OP PROFIT | 38 | 8.7 | 42 | 10.0 | 38 | 9.3 | 97 | 6.3 | 153 | 9.6 | 118 | 7.9 |
| | | | | | | | | | | | | |
| TOTAL FTEs | 22 | | | | 21 | | 21 | | | | 21 | |
| PROF PER TOTAL FTE | 20 | | | | 22 | | 14 | | | | 17 | |
| RET ON CAP. EMPLOYED | 26 % | | | | 29 % | | 19 % | | | | 23 % | |
| COS/TOTAL FTE | 84 | | | | 84 | | 86 | | | | 79 | |

WORKING CAPITAL

| STOCKS | MONTH END | | CORE |
|---|---|---|---|
| | £'000s | WKS | WKS |
| TIMBER | 77 | 13 | 7 |
| SHEET MTLS | 14 | 5 | 5 |
| JOINERY | 31 | 9 | 5 |
| MATERIALS | 135 | 6 | 7 |
| FITTINGS | 23 | 5 | 7 |
| | 280 | 38 | |

| | JAN | FEB | MAR | APR | MAY | JUN | JUL | AUG | SEP | OCT | NOV | DEC | AVG |
|---|---|---|---|---|---|---|---|---|---|---|---|---|---|
| DEBTOR DAYS THIS Yr. | 67 | 66 | 58 | #REF! | | | | | | | | | #REF! |

Here is a building supplies retailer; just look at how much useful management information can be compressed into one sheet of paper. Information about volumes, margins, costs, customers, and even working capital, have found their way onto a single piece of paper. Although it still shows its profit and loss account roots, you can see that the whole suite has been carefully prepared and thought through.

Not only are there volume and profit measures, but room is found for debtors and stock information. Additionally there are the beginnings of more clever things such as Key Performance Indicators (KPIs), profit per employee and so on.

You may also get the impression that business indulges in key performance indicators, league tabling, and ritual public humiliation. But it works!

Now all of this hasn't come about by accident. What you need to do is to sit down with your managers who will use the information. Get some flipcharts and brainstorm the performance measures that they, the users (managers), would value. Notice how the sheet is headed up by the 'tree of ratios', to give a framework to 'anchor' the discussions.

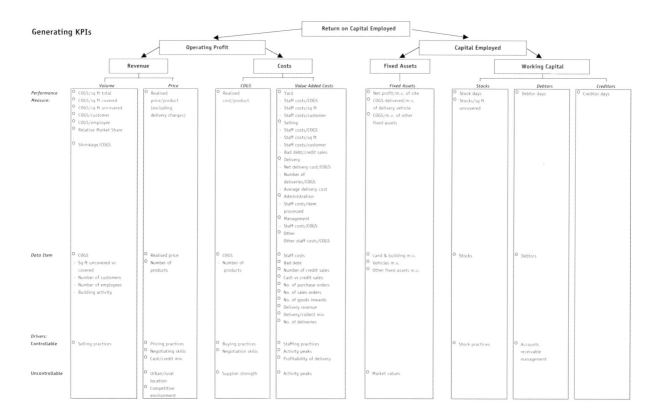

| Performance Area | Branch Performance | | Comparative Branches | |
| --- | --- | --- | --- | --- |
| | First half this year (ann) £000s | Full year this year (ann) £000s | Upper Quartile | Profit Improvement Opportunity |
| **Sales Productivity** | | | | |
|     COS/Ex stock FTEs | £0.0 | £0.0 | £0.0 | £0.0 |
|     COS/customer | £0.0 | £0.0 | £0.0 | £0.0 |
| **Pricing** | | | | |
|     Gross margin | 0.0% | 0.0% | 0.0% | £0.0 |
| **Branch Cost Control** | | | | |
|     Staff costs/Ex stock COS | 0.0% | 0.0% | 0.0% | £0.0 |
|     FTE/Ex stock COS | 0.0 | 0.0 | 0.0 | £0.0 |
|     Other branch costs/Ex stock COS | 0.0% | 0.0% | 0.0% | £0.0 |
|     Delivery costs/COS delivered | 0.0% | 0.0% | 0.0% | £0.0 |
| **Stock Management** | | | | |
|     Stock weeks | 0.0 | 0.0 | 0.0 | £0.0 |
| **Debtor Control** | | | | |
|     Debtor days - average | 0 | 0 | 0 | £0.0 |
|     Debtor days - end of period | 0 | 0 | 0 | £0.0 |
| **Net Profit £000/FTE** | £0.0 | £0.0 | £0.0 | £0.0 |
| **Net Margin** | 0.0% | 0.0% | 0.0% | £0.0 |
| **Net return on capital employed** | 0.0% | 0.0% | 0.0% | £0.0 |

Once you have got this, then you have the small issue that your accounting systems are really nothing more than an invoice adding machine, so in order to provide this useful management information you may well need a completely new set of systems. Such is the price that you may have to pay.

Once you have this cracked, then the rest should be quite straightforward and at last you have a chance of obtaining the holy grail of forward-looking useful management information. See how the company that we have already looked at used the information they measured to give forward-looking pointers.

They take the most important key performance indicators and show what an individual branch could have obtained ('Profit Improvement Opportunity') if only they had been able to achieve the upper quartile in each KPI.

## Balanced business scorecard

Probably the best known and trendy tool being used at the moment is Kaplan's Balanced Business Scorecard (BBS). Just as it is clearly not right to just measure a business on the financials, neither is any other one indicator sufficient.

Instead the BBS suggests a holistic approach, and there are four cornerstones. These all need measuring to a greater or lesser degree, it is argued.

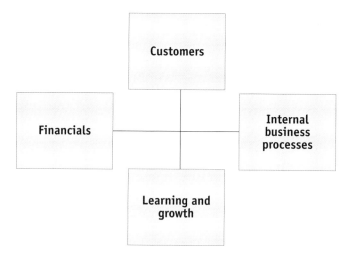

Very briefly, the BBS suggests that all the following items, where relevant to you, should be measured.

- **Customers:** are we pleasing them, are they coming back, have we got new ones, what do they really want from us, what market share do we have and so on?

- **Internal businesses processes:** what internal things do we need to do and manage better in order to give the customer what they want?

- **Learning and growth:** are we as individuals and as an organisation equipped to deal with both the customer and internal business process demands if not, then what do we need to set about doing now to ensure that we are competent?

- **Financials:** apart from the traditional financial measures, we need to consider measuring other items, but mainly financial performance is probably best considered as simply an outcome of getting the other three measures right.

Actually, from what I have seen, there is nothing fundamentally new in the BBS – much of the thinking has been around for some time. It is, in my experience, an extremely useful tool for business measurement and performance improvement. On the simplest level, once you have thought out the indicators within each box, not only do you have your management information suite – you also have your strategic plan and budget prepared!

# Costs

# Chapter 6

## Introduction

We are now going to look at one of the most important areas of finance that a business encounters on a regular basis – that of costing. By costing I mean all those activities which, taken together, gives rise to the business's view of exactly how much each of its products or services cost, and therefore how much each should therefore be sold for.

Now although this sounds easy it is staggering how often people just plainly get it wrong. Who can forget BMC (they used to make the Mini in the 1960s) as they sold each Mini for less than the manufacturing cost. You wouldn't think that you could get that sort of thing wrong, but people do. And, importantly, size has nothing to do with it either; generally the bigger the organisation, the bigger the mistake. The whole of the annual production multiplies a simple error up, and the company is brought to its knees. Sophisticated costing systems conspire to create a black hole of financial truth, where none but the supposedly costing literate dares to venture. Those managers who may have an inkling that all is not well with the costs are excluded by jargon and witchcraft, and so the errors continue.

*Key Question*

So, what should you be aware of to make your life easier and your business healthier? Let us first look at costs and break-even points in an altogether duller context as the traditional break-even chart.

# Break-even

## Break-even charts

The two diagrams below have the following axes: along the horizontal we trace the volume of activity in the business (more sales), and along the vertical axis we trace £ (£ cost as well as £ income).

Now, what does a fixed cost line look like on the chart? Remember that a fixed cost is one that does not change in total £s with increased (or decreased) volume of activity. So, yes, it should be a horizontal line. In diagram 1, the fixed costs are set as being high, whereas in diagram 2 they are set as being low. Can you begin to imagine what type of business each diagram will represent, or which one more closely resembles your own business?

**Diagram 1**

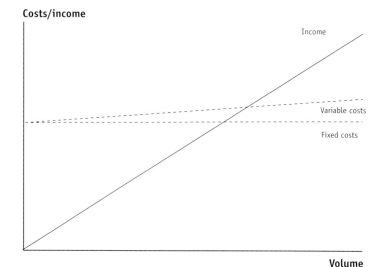

Next, the variable costs. These increase/decrease in line with the volume of activity, and so will slope up as volumes increase. The gradient of the slope will depend upon the amount of the variable cost itself; a higher variable cost will have a steeper gradient.

**Diagram 2**

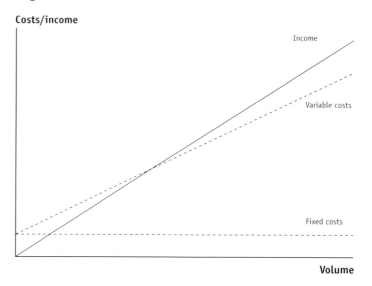

On the diagrams the variable cost lines are shown. Diagram 1, which has higher fixed costs, will have lower variable costs. The opposite applies to diagram 2; it has lower fixed costs and will therefore have higher variable costs. We will start the variable cost line just above the fixed cost line, so that we have a visual representation of the total costs within the business.

## Bringing businesses to life

Now, try to name a well-known business that fits each scenario. Start with the business structure represented in diagram 1. Think of a business with high fixed and low variable costs.

The answer should be most businesses with the word British in the name – British Airways, Telecom, Gas and so on. These are the classic examples of high fixed, low variable cost businesses. Try looking at it this way: what is the marginal (incremental) cost of British Rail putting you on a train? The answer is, of course, pretty close to nil.

More difficult is the business with lower fixed costs but higher variable costs. You can almost think of this as representing the 'virtual', subcontracted or outsourced business. See what is happening at the BBC (that shoots the 'British...' argument, above, in the foot) where they have seriously reduced the full-time headcount. Much of the content is now produced by third parties, not the BBC themselves, as can be seen by the appearance of non-BBC logos at the end of programmes. Interestingly, the BBC has extended the already existing trend of outsourcing parts of its business. Let's examine this further.

## Outsourcing

One of the ways that we can see the use of break-even principles in practice is to look at the recently popularised trend of outsourcing. Businesses take a long hard look at all that they do, and decide that a third party could better do some of the 'non-core' activities. Common examples across the business spectrum have been IT, facilities management and transport and distribution. The debate runs like this. Sainsbury's, for example, simply say that they are grocers (par excellence, of course), and not information technology experts or motor mechanics. The amount of time, space, training and resources given currently to these functions internally could be better spent on having a third party providing a higher quality, more cost-effective service. It is this perceived gain in both cost and quality that is usually sufficient to tip the balance in favour of outsourcing. Or, to put it more bluntly in hard financial terms, the replacement of previously fixed costs by now variable costs, even at a greater cost, will be tolerated provided there are gains in quality.

The problem with this trend has, and always will be, the management of the supposed gains of cost and quality. Take that with the suggestion that there really is nothing that can't be outsourced and you begin to realise what the business of the future might well look like.

## Finance out

The latest function to follow the trend is, somewhat surprisingly to many people, finance and accounting. Whilst a business will always need a core of head office accountants to comply with the essential reporting functions, there is no real reason why the rest can't be done elsewhere. Indeed, there are compelling reasons why it should be done elsewhere. One of the typical weaknesses inside any business is the overall level of management information available to managers to help them make decisions. There is, on the other hand, a plethora of traditional backward-looking profit and loss accounts with variance analyses – a P and L account 'dump' as it is known in the trade. If you're lucky you might get a balance sheet, and if you're really lucky you might get a cash flow statement. Really useful information may be tacked on or shoehorned into available spaces on various reports.

## Risk and reward

Back to the break-even chart, and we can see that the pictures do indeed describe differently structured business types, or even describe different parts of the same business. For example, certain departments/functions may be in-house (fixed) or outsourced (variable).

If we now overlay on both diagrams the line that represents sales income (sloping up, left to right), of the same gradient on each diagram, you can see two key things.

Firstly the point at which income is equal to total costs is called the break-even point. This point is lower in diagram 2 than 1; in other words business two breaks-even at a lower volume than business one. This is sometimes referred to as the 'sleep easy at night' business. Put another way, if you were starting your own business from scratch, you would not immediately employ several people (all with an Audi A4), rent city centre premises and then sit back and wait for sales to arrive (the high fixed cost route). You would probably work from home, sub-contract out work you did not have the capacity to do yourself, and take things one step at a time (the low fixed cost route).

## Break-even points

I should point out that the calculation of a break-even point is, in many people's minds, one of the most important things to be done when getting a feel for figures. Here is how to do it. To calculate a break-even point in terms of £ sales, you need to take the fixed costs of whatever it is that you are looking at, and divide by a gross margin.

*Key Learning Point*

Take as an example a business about to employ a sales person for a gross salary cost of £25,000 per annum. Once you have added on the national insurance, travel, hotels, petrol and so on we could easily be talking about a total employment cost of around £50,000.

Assuming that the gross margin the business does on average is around 20%, then the break-even point calculation will be £50,000 divided by 0.20, which gives £250,000.

This means that for the business to start to make any money at all it needs to do incremental sales of £250,000. Perhaps this is a very far cry from the manager of the department looking at his original budget and seeing that he had £25,000 to spend on a salesman.

Many poor decisions are being made by businesses every day, where the total cost of making a decision and, more importantly, the sales needed to justify taking on that extra cost, simply are not being made. Unless and until people appreciate that the incremental sales are what justifies taking on extra cost, businesses will continue to go backwards. Please use this technique whenever you are considering taking on additional costs, and remember that the business with the lower break-even point will last longer.

For the calculation of a whole business break-even point, refer back to the example when we did the financial analysis and cash flow statement.

## Life is not all straight lines

*Activity*

Just to show that life is not as simple as straight lines might have you believe, here is an example to show non-linear demand and its effect upon selling and pricing decisions. Simply fill in the blanks in the information below. You can see for yourself how the curvilinear demand function will provide an optimum price.

Fred buys and sells second-hand books. He is considering changing their pricing policy that currently is to sell books at 70% of the new book price. It is believed that reducing the price to 40% of the new book price will treble sales. However, before a final decision is made the following data has been gathered to assist with the decision.

| | |
|---|---|
| Number of books sold per year | 16,000 |
| Average 'new book price' | £10.00 |
| Average cost to Discount Bookshop | £2.20 |
| Average selling price (at present) | £7.00 |
| Fixed costs per year | £40,000 |
| Other variable costs (average per book sold) | £0.10 |

Estimated effect of reducing selling prices:

| Average selling price | Books sold per year |
|---|---|
| £7.00 | 16,000 |
| £6.00 | 23,000 |
| £5.00 | 33,000 |
| £4.00 | 48,000 |
| £3.00 | 80,000 |

What pricing policy do you recommend? Fill in the following table.

| Average selling price | Contribution per book | Books sold per year | Contribution per year |
|---|---|---|---|
| £7.00 | | | |
| £6.00 | | | |
| £5.00 | | | |
| £4.00 | | | |
| £3.00 | | | |

Maximum contribution (and profit) occurs at
an average selling price of                    £ _____

At which profit =                              £ _____ per year

Your answer should look something like this:

| Average selling price | Contribution per book | Books sold per year | Contribution per year |
|---|---|---|---|
| £7.00 | £4.70 | 16,000 | £75,200 |
| £6.00 | £3.70 | 23,000 | £85,100 |
| £5.00 | £2.70 | 33,000 | £89,100 |
| £4.00 | £1.70 | 48,000 | £81,600 |
| £3.00 | £0.70 | 80,000 | £56,000 |

Maximum contribution (and profit) occurs at an average selling price of £5.00    £ 89,100

At which profit =    £ 59,100 per year

Let's now move on from break-even points to the finer elements of costs.

# Building up costs

We have already looked at the building blocks of costs – fixed and variable. How do we put this principle of cost classification into practice? Here is a quick example that we all encounter, namely how to set a selling price for goods and services.

From first principles, if you were asked to set a selling price, how in reality would you do it? Would you do as we are about to do (building up a model of costs, then adding profit), or would you simply look to see what the opposition is doing?

Typically we tend to do the latter, if only as a sense check at first – but that quickly becomes the standard 'we can't possibly charge that much more/less than the opposition'.

## Menu pricing

Anyway, back to this simple little build-up example with figures. Here is the scene. You run a business dealing with motor car repairs and servicing. With the aid of three employees, you reckon that a total of 6,000 hours per year could be used effectively for repairs and service work. The following budgeted information is available for the coming year.

| | |
|---|---|
| Total staff costs | £42,000 |
| Rent and rates | £5,000 |
| Depreciation of equipment | £9,300 |
| Electricity, gas and telephone | £2,500 |
| Advertising costs | £2,700 |
| Parts, materials, oils, etc. | £45,000 |

What you want to do is work out a simple costing structure to enable you to make a profit, and to be used to cost jobs. Let's start first with the labour cost per effective hour. To calculate this you need to take the annual labour cost and divide by the annual effective hours.

| | | |
|---|---|---|
| Annual labour cost | = | £ 42,000 per annum |
| Annual effective hours | = | 6,000 hours per annum |
| Labour cost per effective hour | = | Labour cost per annum |
| | | ——————————— |
| | | Effective hours per annum |
| | = | £42,000 |
| | | —————— |
| | | 6,000 |
| | = | £ 7.00 per hour |

## Total costing pitfalls

This gives a pretty understandable first estimate; if we sell all the 6,000 hours of labour time then we will need to charge at least £7.00 per hour just to cover the cost of that labour. Profit will need to be added on top. However, the point of this example is to demonstrate the fundamental problem in using this approach (often called the 'Total' or 'Absorbtion' costing system) whereby total costs, both fixed and variable, are included in computing a theoretical future selling price. If you just think about the important assumption we have just made, that we will sell all the available labour hours, and the impact on the business this should not be the case. What, for example, would happen if we were to sell only 5,000 hours of labour? The answer is that we would not be charging enough per hour to cover our labour costs, or under-recovering. What about the opposite case, when we are fortunate enough to sell 7,000 hours of labour? The answer is that we would be charging too much to cover our labour costs; or over-recovering, and possibly looking expensive against our competitors.

On such simple assumptions can the total costing system stand or fall. Its accuracy nearly always depends upon the accuracy and validity of the initial assumption about volume (volume of activity, in this case labour hours).

## Overheads

Let's now move on to the next set of costs in the business, the overheads. Specifically, the question is what is the overhead cost per effective hour to cover the cost of rent, rates, depreciation, electricity, gas, telephone and advertising? We usually apply the same treatment and spread the total of these other costs over the same assumed volume that we have already seen in the first example (thereby perpetuating the potential error introduced by making an assumption about the labour hours volume, and so on).

Total overheads (exclude parts, materials, oils, etc.) per year

$$= £ 19,500 \text{ per annum}$$

$$\text{Overhead cost per effective hour} = \frac{\text{Total overheads per annum}}{\text{Effective hours per annum}}$$

$$= \frac{£19,500}{6,000}$$

$$= £ 3.25 \text{ per hour}$$

Usually the two elements are now added together to arrive at the gross labour cost per effective hour (for labour plus overhead).

| Gross labour cost per effective hour | = | Labour cost per effective hour + Overhead cost per effective hour |
|---|---|---|
| | = | £ 7.00 per hour + £ 3.25 per hour |
| | = | £ 10.25 per hour |

We have now arrived at, under our accepted costing convention adopted in this case, a formula by which we may establish the cost (and hence selling price) for any job that the business undertakes.

For example, what is the price paid by the customer for six hours of labour time and £15 worth (at cost) of parts? Assume that we usually add 20% to labour, overheads and parts to provide for financial charges and profit.

| Total cost | = | (Labour hours x Gross Labour Rate per hour) + costs of parts |
|---|---|---|
| | = | (6 hrs x £10.25/hr) + £15.00 |
| | = | £76.50 |
| Add mark-up of 20% | = | £76.50 + £15.30 |
| | | £91.80 |

## Mark-up and margin

*Key Learning Point*

As an aside to the costing and pricing issue, are you sure that you understand mark-up as opposed to margin? I have seen a business which was supposed to make a 15% margin on sales, and yet the staff were simply marking up their purchases by 15%. They were genuinely surprised when they got their knuckles rapped for not meeting profit targets! Here is a simple way to look at the situation.

The first point to grasp is one of terminology: mark-up applies to cost price, whereas margin applies to selling price.

The second point is the mathematical relationship between the two terms which throws up an interesting, and not often understood, relationship. Here is an example of someone who buys an item for £100 and then marks it up by 25% (or £25). We could write this as:

```
Cost price +        Profit = Selling price
     £100 +          £25 =         £125
              Represents
              mark-up of
                 25% (or 1/4)
```

Alternatively we could establish the same £ of profit by looking from the 'other end of the telescope', from selling price. This perspective shows that we have made £25 of profit on sales of £125, which represents a margin of 20%.

```
Cost price +        Profit = Selling price
     £100 +          £25 =         £125
              Represents
              margin of
                 20% (or 1/5)
```

Our conclusions are therefore:

1) A 20% margin (£25) is not the same as a 20% mark-up (this would be equal to a profit of £20) in our example above. This can explain why many businesses are told to mark-up bought in third party services for clients by a strange figure such as 17.65% – until you realise that a 17.65% mark-up is equal to a 15% margin. Check it for yourself!

2) A $^1/_5$ margin is equal to a $^1/_4$ mark-up, a $^1/_4$ margin is equal to a $^1/_3$ mark-up, a $^1/_3$ margin is equal to a $^1/_2$ mark-up, and so on.

## Marginal versus total costing

Back to costing, now, and we had got as far as examining the total costing model. The alternative to the total costing model is the marginal (or variable) costing model. This simply ignores fixed costs (about which we have to make often flawed assumptions about volume of activity over which to spread the fixed costs) and looks only at variable costs. The picture is altogether much less complicated, and the differences can be summed up in the following checklist of differences.

*Action Checklist*

|  | **TOTAL COSTING** | **MARGINAL COSTING** |
|---|---|---|
| **Advantages** | Shows the total cost of product<br><br>Identifies product profitability | Easy to understand<br><br>Makes budgeting and variance analysis easier |
| **Disadvantages** | Difficult to understand, complicated and time-consuming to prepare, subjective<br><br>Can become out of date | Confusion of contribution and profit, sometimes sell at below true total cost<br><br>Emphasises short-term results |

The real advantages of marginal costing can be seen in this checklist – we simply don't have to worry about the often confusing, inestimable and uncontrollable things that are fixed costs and other overheads. After all, provided we carry on making things at a marginal profit (selling price exceeds variable costs of making that extra thing), then we can't go far wrong, can we?

## Comprehensive example

Well, we can go wrong. As the list suggests, there are some difficulties in focusing on marginal costing alone. To illustrate the point, here is another worked example. This time the business is couched in the more mundane surroundings of a fish and chip shop. The shop sells fried fish and chips, fish cakes, sausages and pasties as well as wet fish, vinegar, sauces, canned soft drinks and other miscellaneous items. The operations look something like this:

| | | |
|---|---:|---:|
| Sales | | |
| Fried fish | | £ 32,000 |
| Chips | | 16,000 |
| Other fried products | | 8,000 |
| Wet fish | | 8,000 |
| Other items | | 8,000 |
| Total sales | | 72,000 |
| Expenses | | |
| Fish for frying | £ 22,400 | |
| Potatoes | 4,800 | |
| Other fried products | 4,800 | |
| Fish sold uncooked | 8,000 | |
| Other items | 6,400 | |
| Frying oil and batter | 1,920 | |
| Frying equipment depreciation | 3,200 | |
| Other equipment depreciation | 800 | |
| Rent, rates, gas and electricity | 5,280 | |
| Total expenses | | 57,600 |
| Profit | | £14,400 |

You ascertain that the following costs are regarded as fixed:

- Depreciation (calculated on a straight line basis);

- Rent and rates, and part of the gas and electricity – £3,200 in total.

Firstly, let's try to ascertain the split of costs between fixed and variable – in other words which costs are volume related (increase overall in direct proportion to output) and which are not (do not increase with volume). The following table shows how the costs should be allocated:

| Expenses | | Variable | Fixed |
|---|---|---|---|
| Fish for frying | £ 22,400 | 22,400 | |
| Potatoes | 4,800 | 4,800 | |
| Other fried products | 4,800 | 4,800 | |
| Fish sold uncooked | 8,000 | 8,000 | |
| Other items | 6,400 | 6,400 | |
| Frying oil and batter | 1,920 | 1,920 | |
| Frying equipment depreciation | 3,200 | | 3,200 |
| Other equipment depreciation | 800 | | 800 |
| Rent, rates, gas and electricity | 5,280 | 2,080 | 3,200 |
| Total expenses | 57,600 | 50,400 | 7,200 |

The only trick here is that the gas and electricity is part fixed, part variable; the other costs are straightforward. Notice how raw materials are generally always variable, whereas depreciation and overheads are generally fixed.

Having split the variable and fixed costs, we can now look at a key concept or sub-total for most management accountants and costing people – contribution. Contribution is defined as being selling price less variable costs. It sounds simple, doesn't it – and it really is very useful, but it does have drawbacks. We will now calculate the contribution for our example:

| Sales | £ 72,000 |
|---|---|
| Less: Variable Costs | 50,400 |
| Contribution | 21,600 |
| Less: Fixed Costs | 7,200 |
| Profit | £ 14,400 |

The real benefit of looking at contribution is that it shows the additional profit made for each additional product sold. In this case the contribution is £21,600 on sales of £72,000 – or 30%. In practice this is a critical figure, since every £1 taken over the counter results on average in 30 pence contribution – or 30 pence towards covering the fixed costs. The real drawback is that slavishly following contribution as a yardstick ignores the other (fixed) costs, and as a consequence people think that contribution is in fact profit; which it clearly isn't.

Contrast this with the traditional financial accountant's view which focuses on gross and net profit.

| | | |
|---|---|---|
| Sales | | £ 72,000 |
| Less: Cost of sales | | 53,600 |
| | Gross Profit | 18,400 |
| Less: Other Costs | | 4,000 |
| | Net Profit | £ 14,400 |

As a diversion – outside the fixed and variable dimension another perspective (and another figure) is the often quoted 'average cost', which really defines itself. The total costs in this example are £57,600, which represent an average cost of 80 pence for every £1 of sales.

## Direct and indirect costs

Now onto another dimension of costing, one that is increasingly important in trying to measure business health: the allocation of costs into direct and indirect. As with all things financial , different businesses often have completely different definitions and usages of the same fundamental words.

So, firstly, we'll deal with the definitions of direct and indirect. Direct costs are those that are incurred solely for the benefit of **one** product or service, whereas indirect costs are incurred for the benefit of **many** products or services (in other words, shared costs). This one-to-many distinction is the key to understanding direct and indirect costs, and any other definition that you may have heard should be ignored.

Now, using the analyses we have already performed, simply place each of the costs into the appropriate box. What you get is a useful indicator as to exactly where the costs lie within your business, and therefore what you could perhaps be doing to manage them more proactively.

Here is the completed box for a fish and chip shop, and you will of course notice that one box is blank – the fixed indirect cost type. What would appear here, within the fish and chip shop scenario? What cost is not volume dependent (fixed) and yet is incurred only for the benefit of a single product or service? You would have to scratch around a bit here, but depreciation on a potato peeler would be good enough!

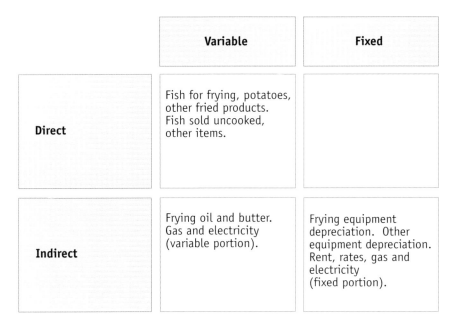

|  | Variable | Fixed |
|---|---|---|
| **Direct** | Fish for frying, potatoes, other fried products. Fish sold uncooked, other items. |  |
| **Indirect** | Frying oil and butter. Gas and electricity (variable portion). | Frying equipment depreciation. Other equipment depreciation. Rent, rates, gas and electricity (fixed portion). |

## Business cost generalisations

As a general note of interest, within most businesses the majority of costs lie along the variable/direct to fixed/indirect axis. Just thinking about this reinforces this finding. The top left box (variable/direct) is essentially raw materials for products, or cost of sales for services. These are not such a problem to control. The bottom right box (fixed/indirect) represent all the centralised/shared costs. Just why are they being incurred, and what can we do to control them better? As businesses get 'smarter' (increasing the use of IT is a good example), it becomes harder to really get a finger on the pulse and control costs and profitability properly. Such are the drawbacks to the way we work now.

*Key Learning Point*

## Product profitability

Now, back to product profitability. Product profitability may be known, as is the case for many concepts, by a variety of different names. It really all depends on which guru or management consultant is peddling the idea at the time, and what handle they have chosen to give it in order to differentiate it from the other similar ideas doing the rounds. The commonest aliases are product profitability, client profitability, and channel profitability – any profitability measure that enables you to get a handle on how well you are doing. Let me put it another way, and use a quick example to illustrate the point.

Take a business that makes or sells just three items. Let's say it is an office equipment supplier whose three main product lines are copiers, printers and faxes. The typical analysed profit and loss account below is not untypical for many businesses, in that the scorekeeping system can cope with the direct costs for each product (typically variable) such as the cost of the goods themselves, carriage, deterioration and so on. What the scorekeeping system cannot cope with is how to allocate or apportion the indirect costs between each product (typically fixed) such as the costs of selling, marketing, administration, finance, personnel, board of directors and so on.

|                         | Copiers | Printers | Faxes | Total |
|-------------------------|---------|----------|-------|-------|
| Sales proceeds          | £ 50    | £ 30     | £ 20  | £ 100 |
| Variable (direct) costs | 30      | 20       | 10    | 60    |
| Contribution            | 20      | 10       | 10    | 40    |
| Fixed (indirect) costs  | ?       | ?        | ?     | 30    |
| Profit                  | ?       | ?        | ?     | £ 10  |

Consequently what we know about is what the contribution (or gross profit) is, but we are completely blind as to whether a product, client or channel is really profitable at the bottom line. Using the figures above, the three products appear to be making a contribution of 40%, 33% and 50% respectively. Using this as a decision-making guideline, we might be tempted to concentrate on faxes, as they appear to be making us the most money (as measured by contribution). But, as we well know, this is only part of the picture. How should we treat the £30 chunk of costs that are fixed (indirect)?

## Typical allocations

What most businesses do is to apportion the fixed (indirect) costs back to the products themselves, and the contribution less the allocated portion of the fixed (indirect) costs then gives product profitability – a genuinely more relevant and useful measure. The real problem, however, is not should we allocate, but how do we allocate? The first point to accept here is that any method of allocation is subjective, arbitrary and open to debate. There really can be no such thing as an entirely accurate allocation or apportionment.

Typically most businesses split according to one of the following, in order of popularity (generally correlates with ease!):

£ Sales value

Sales units

£ Cost of sales

£ Contribution

Headcount

Floor area

There are, of course, many more ways of doing the splits; it all depends how imaginative you want to be, and how much time you have to spare. Do remember, though, that this exercise does not, in itself, make the business any more money; it merely spreads the blame for what has already happened, and thereby hopes to provide better quality information for making decisions in the future.

Consider the reality of the situation within the four walls of the office equipment supplier. How should management allocate the fixed (indirect) costs? Let's take the commonest of the allocation methods described above, £ sales value.

|                        | Copiers | Printers | Faxes | Total |
|------------------------|---------|----------|-------|-------|
| Sales proceeds         | £ 50    | £ 30     | £ 20  | £ 100 |
| Variable (direct) costs | 30      | 20       | 10    | 60    |
| Contribution           | 20      | 10       | 10    | 40    |
| Fixed (indirect) costs | 15      | 9        | 6     | 30    |
| Profit                 | £ 5     | £ 1      | £ 4   | £ 10  |

If we do this, we see that copiers and faxes make profits, but that printers hardly seem worth it just for a paltry £1 profit. So what could we conclude: that printers is not a profitable market to be in? That's what our analysis seems to be telling us, and it seems well reasoned and argued. So, let's drop printers and just focus on copiers and faxes.

Now, that might very well be the right answer, but I doubt it. Perhaps another way of looking at it is this. Will we, in withdrawing from printers, realistically drop £9 of fixed indirect cost (or 9/30ths of the total of fixed indirect cost)? Will we, for example, lose selling and marketing costs, or 9/30ths of the finance function costs, or 9/30ths of the board of directors' cost? It does sound rather unlikely, doesn't it, yet the logic that got us there in the first place is undeniable.

## Typical conclusions

So, what we have so far in real life is a sorry procession of businesses that do the following:

- Apportion costs in a 'finger in the wind' manner, bearing no resemblance to reality, then

- Believe the apparent product profitability figures that are produced, then

- Withdraw from the product whose profitability appears lowest, then

- Throw their hands up in amazement when, next year, the profitability of the remaining business looks even worse than before taking that painful decision.

## New good, old bad?

Does this sound familiar, and how has it happened in your business? There is a saying for these businesses, and it goes like this:

*'Businesses consistently underestimate the profitability of existing products, and overestimate the profitability of new products'.*

Now, I guarantee that is familiar.

It's not really surprising, especially when you consider what happens in real life. As a first example, take an electrical superstore retailer that has been selling fridges, cookers and so on for years, but is now into the computer market. Just how long do you think it takes a salesman to sell a fridge or cooker? Probably around five or ten minutes on average. Compare that to how long it takes to sell the latest computer to a rampaging family of five: its, more like a one hour question and answer session mixed with a lecture. Do you think that the product profitability figures reflect this reality of how costs are driven – or, guess what, will it be a sales volume split again? Of course it will.

## Activity based costing

Now there is a better way (many, actually, but one is well known and peddled), and it's called ABC, or Activity Based Costing. What ABC does is that it gets you to guess the allocation a little more accurately. Remember what we discussed earlier: that no allocation could ever be entirely correct. Typically most businesses find that the 80/20 rule applies here. They can allocate better (using ABC) about 80% of the costs in about 20% of the time, but to get that last 20% to achieve perfect allocation will take an unavailable length of time, so be happy with 80%. In reality this last 20% relates to the board of directors, head office and so on, for whom allocation rarely makes any sense at all.

*Key Management Concept*

What happens in an ABC exercise is something like this, and we'll prolong the office equipment retailer example just a little longer. An ABC exercise will probably entail the whole staff in the business keeping detailed timesheets of activity for a representative period of, say, two months. Salesmen, administrators, switchboard operators and accountants will all be recording how they spend their time (by product, channel, client or however you choose). At the same time all costs are recorded in a manner that the product, channel, client or however you choose, will be matched up.

At the end of the ABC period everything that has moved or breathed (on the cost and time front) will have been accurately and faithfully recorded, so allocation should be made easy! Now you can find out exactly how marketing spend their time, and it probably won't be on existing products, more likely to be new launches and the like. It's all very logical and believable, some would say they do something akin to this anyway, without the fancy initials. It is of course critical to the health and future prosperity of your business to know whether your clients and products are providing you with profits or simply a warm (but unprofitable) glow of sales volume and market share, and if they are, then which ones. It might sound surprising to a person in the street, but most businesses simply have no idea about this whole area, preferring simply to navigate on gut feeling! 'Work smarter, not harder', and 'Busy fools' could almost have been invented specifically for these ostrich types of business, who really would rather not know what is going on out there.

## Drawbacks to ABC

Now, there is of course a counter argument, which has two strands. Firstly, of course new products will have greater costs in the initial stages – to say anything else is wrong. Secondly, if you took ABC *ad extremis*, you would never launch any new product, but prefer simply to milk existing rich seams of profit. Both of these counters are, of course, correct. But, where ABC really scores is in its ability to give a business a cold shower of reality about where it is now, and where it might go in the future, and that is its real value.

# Decision-making

We are now going to explore the whole field of decision-making; future looking decision-making at that. Now, you may ask why is it necessary to make such a song and dance about decisions 'in the future', as opposed to 'in the past', and here might be a useful time to introduce the concept of forward or backward looking points of view.

## Backwards and forwards

Look at the following diagram and clear your mind of everything except financial matters. Let's firstly label up the axes. The X (horizontal) axis describes the time frame: right hand is the future, so left hand is the past. The Y (vertical) axis describes whether the person we are describing works inside (top) or outside (bottom) the organisation.

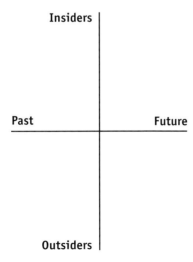

## Inside and outside

Next we simply try to describe a financially oriented person who might fit within each of the four sectors. Where, for example would you put your external auditor? How about a management consultant? And, crucially, what about your internal finance and accounting function; where do they fit (and perhaps, where should they fit)? I bet that, whilst they might self-assess themselves as being half backward and half forward-looking (sitting on the fence again), you would probably place them firmly in the top left-hand box.

```
                        Insiders

        Accounts department │ Financial management

                  Past ────────────────── Future

                    Auditor │ Consultant

                        Outsiders
```

What you can see is that the 'traditional' tasks and roles of accountants and financial experts are generally backward facing. This is not really all that surprising, since we all prefer to be dealing with the certainty of what has actually come to pass and happened (no matter how subjectively and creatively we might then account for those events!) rather than try to predict and quantify future and as yet uncertain events.

## Brave new world

Actually, this picture has another story to tell us, and it's all rather tribal or sectarian, mixed in with different languages and customs. Empirical study shows us that the backward-looking people actually use a different language and set of measures to the forward-looking people. Each tribe views the other with considerable suspicion. It has always been like this between financial and management accountants.

However there is no smoke without fire, and there is more than a grain of truth to this debate. In spite of having spent the better part of this book explaining how a working understanding of traditional finance and accounting can be a fulfiling and uplifting experience, I am now going to suggest that you throw this all away and learn a new language. Indeed in this brave new future-facing world of financial decision-making the old craft is woefully inadequate. See what you think about it all at the end of this topic – some people feel that they are actually doing no more than swapping the traditional uncertainties (creative accounting, flexibility, subjectivity) for an equally daunting and friable set of alternative uncertainties (predictability, forecasts, estimates, assumptions). Don't let me sway you one way or another, though. The important thing is to appreciate how little (if at all) we will refer to the traditional financial accounting baggage and terminology, just watch.

## Winds of change

The final overlay on the diagram is the 'Winds of Change'. The prevailing south westerlies are driving the areas of expected financial competence up from the bottom left to the top right corner; the trouble is, do accountants have the necessary skills to enable them to live with the demands and expectations in this box?

So, we will start on this future-facing journey by looking at a simple first example. You are faced with the following opportunity, and have to decide whether to go ahead with the initiative, or not. Take all the information at face value, and don't try to overcomplicate matters. Assume that the opportunity has a duration of just one year, that should make it easy enough.

## Decision time – case study

Trinket Toys are considering launching a new model kit version of the Jaguar XK120 car for sale primarily in the domestic market. They have already undertaken market research with ToyPR, the leading toy research agency, at a cost of £100,000 which indicates that the product should be commercially viable, reaching sales of 250,000 units at a selling price of £2 a time.

The product would necessitate amendments to the production line costing £100,000 and variable costs of production of £350,000 covering all material, labour and production costs.

Do you think that the project should be undertaken?

| | | |
|---|---|---|
| Sales | | £500,000 |
| Cost of sales | | 350,000 |
| | *gross* | 150,000 |
| Amendments | | 100,000 |
| | *net* | 50,000 |
| Research | | 100,000 |
| | *net* | -£50,000 |

From the above table it looks like the result is negative £50,000, so the answer is that it probably isn't worth doing. Accordingly we would shelve the project. However the alternative approach is frequently taken: 'But look at all the money we've spent so far, of course we must continue'. A typical, but flawed, rallying cry. All the accountants in the world weep silently and gnash their teeth at the absurdity of the decision.

## Look forward

The correct decision is, of course, to go ahead with the project. Why? The key to this puzzle is the market research expenditure, which has already been spent. Since it has already been spent it really cannot form any part of the decision-making you are about to undertake. We call this type of cost a 'Sunk Cost', and it must always be ignored.

It may be hard to accept this, and indeed it may run counter to whatever your business tells you that you should be doing (in which case they are in the wrong), but it is correct. Simply ask the following question: 'If we were to decide not to go ahead with the project, would the market research company refund us the money we have already spent with them?' Of course they wouldn't, and nothing illustrates the point about sunk costs better. The financial 'line' for making the correct decision will therefore look like this: a £50,000 positive as opposed to a £50,000 negative seen earlier.

| | | |
|---|---|---|
| Sales | | £500,000 |
| Cost of sales | | 350,000 |
| | *gross* | 150,000 |
| Amendments | | 100,000 |
| | *net* | £50,000 |

It is interesting to note that, whilst most people instinctively should appreciate this point about sunk costs being irrelevant, somehow they just can't seem to help themselves. A very real and commonplace occurrence goes like this. You have prepared a watertight project appraisal, and the figures look good, but there isn't exactly a lot of slack. You submit them for review to your accountant who then apparently from nowhere spirits up several costs that have already been paid which he can conveniently attach to your embryonic project. A memo comes back to you with words to the effect that 'It doesn't look too good now, does it, with all these extra costs?' And you are defeated. In actual fact, all the business is in danger of doing is turning down perfectly feasible opportunities because of flawed computations; you are right, so stick to your guns!

This is actually a very interesting exercise to give to your staff. Typically answers are split half-and-half; do/don't do. Show it to your accountant as well, and see what answer you get!

# Golden rules for decisions

## Sunk costs

So, if we were to draw up a list of Golden Rules for decision making, the first one would be:

> 1. Ignore Sunk Costs

How many of you have already made the next leap, which is to associate fixed costs with sunk costs; in other words, aren't all fixed costs sunk? Think about it more closely. If you are about to undertake a project, any fixed cost within the business is already committed and decided upon without your project, and therefore cannot be associated with it (sunk). It's all quite simple, really, provided you use logic and not raw accounting blame-allocating emotion.

It is now the time to introduce a heading to our list of Golden Rules. I have so far spoken only about 'costs for decision-making', but what they really should be called is 'relevant costs'.

## Relevant costs

So far, therefore, we have seen that a sunk cost is not a relevant cost. What other costs should we be including or excluding? The next definition to get our heads around is the one for 'Opportunity' costs, which are sometimes known as 'Incremental' costs; but to normal human beings neither word encourages an instant definition to exactly leap off the page!

## Incremental or opportunity

Fundamentally this term is supposed to catch only those costs which increase (or decrease, the point being that they do in fact change) as a direct result of something taking place, hence the term incremental. The dimension usually put upon this is the 'business as a whole'. Let me give some examples.

Assume that you are about to do something that will entail using two people for a month. If there are no people available internally to staff up this project, then you will have to buy in some people from outside: full or part time. This cost is a true incremental or opportunity cost to the business as a whole, and therefore is relevant.

If, however, in doing the project you found that there were people available internally and you chose to use them, then there is no incremental or opportunity cost to the business as a whole. Again, whilst the theory of this might sound utterly logical, here is how many businesses make mistakes.

Assuming the latter case (there were people available internally and you chose to use them – no incremental or opportunity cost to the business as a whole) you do your project calculations and submit them for approval. Back comes a memo from the accountant saying 'You have omitted to include a charge for labour at our standard £50 per hour rate'. If you did include this rate, the project wouldn't be worth doing, and yet you know there is no real incremental labour cost, so why on earth is your project being saddled with it? The answer, I'm afraid is ignorance. It is a standard response to apply this kind of 'charge' internally, when clearly there is no 'cost' to the business as a whole. This is a common error perpetrated by most businesses. What they are really confusing, however, is the criteria for decision-making with the need to apportion out costs subsequently; yet the two are entirely different. Do you remember the market research we saw in an earlier example? The cost of that was sunk, and therefore not relevant for decision-making, but that won't stop an accountant from pinning the blame of it into some department's profit and loss account.

To help you look at this in the correct light, here is a visual representation of how to get it right. Imagine a waterproof (or osmotic) barrier around a business. This represents the point which, if crossed, will trigger a cost as being an opportunity or incremental cost; and therefore relevant. Extending the logic would indicate that anything which just shuffles around within the business and does not cross the barrier couldn't therefore be an opportunity or incremental cost.

Not understanding this simple principle is one of the main reasons why businesses undertake unfeasible projects, or on the other hand why they often turn down feasible projects: because the wrong costs are scored as relevant or not relevant. Adding to the Golden Rule list gives us the following so far:

Relevant Costs

     1. Ignore Sunk Costs

     2. Only count Incremental or Opportunity Costs

## A worthwhile opportunity?

Let's now try to put this relevant cost idea into practice with a slightly more involved example.

Dorridge Flying Club Limited, a small friendly business, owns a fleet of six Piper Tomahawk training aircraft which are hired by the hour to members of the public for individual flying practice or for lessons with a qualified instructor.

The management is considering whether they should lease three further aircraft, and they have asked you to help. After a day at the club talking to members of the committee and people who are employed by the club you have ascertained the following facts:

1. At present the club has 2,000 'customers' comprising student pilots and people who already have their private pilot's licence. There is an annual subscription of £10.

2. It has been estimated that if three further aircraft are leased there could be as much as a 25% increase in the number of customers.

3. For a pilot to maintain his licence he must complete at least ten flying hours per year. A student pilot completes about 20 hours of flying with an instructor per year.

4. The lists for booking aircraft open each Monday morning to cover bookings for the following Sunday to Saturday period. The telephone lines are jammed solid for most of Monday.

5. The revenue from an aircraft is £42 per hour and the variable costs for the business (comprising fuel, landing fees and CAA air-worthiness checks) are £38 per hour. On average each plane is in the air for seven hours per day, every day of the year.

6. Fixed overheads of £9,000 comprise the hire of a hanger which accommodates the present six aircraft (but which can house up to nine aircraft) and the maintenance of the aircraft.

7. The additional depreciation charge per aircraft will amount to £800.

8. The cost of leasing is £12,000 per aircraft per annum payable at the end of each year.

**Should the directors lease the additional three aircraft?**

Well, where do we start? This is a slightly simplistic view of life, and as with other examples seen so far do try to take the information at face value and assume that the project should be viewed with a one year horizon. We will not try to be too clever with the projections and assumptions, especially about capacity. We will, however, simply go down the list of points (1 to 8) and decide one by one as to whether the item each describes is, or is not, a relevant cost.

The really important thing is to have a parrot on your shoulder constantly squawking the words 'If were we to go ahead and lease three further aircraft, would this point give rise to additional cost or revenue to the business as a whole?' In other words, do not wrongly omit or wrongly double count any of the items.

| **Point Number** | **£** |
|---|---|
| 1. This merely describes the current situation regarding members and subscription levels. Taken on its own, there is no additional cost or revenue from this information alone were we to go ahead and lease three further aircraft. | **Nil** |
| 2. This is relevant, the implication being that were we to go ahead with the project and lease three further aircraft, then we could expect increased subscription amounts of 25%. 25% of 2,000 'customers' at an annual subscription of £10 equals £5,000. | **5,000** |
| 3. Irrelevant. | |
| 4. Irrelevant. | |
| 5. With revenue of £42 per hour and variable costs of £38 per hour, contribution is £4 per hour. Multiply this up by seven hours per day, 365 days of the year, times three aircraft and you get £30,660 additional income. | **30,660** |
| 6. Irrelevant. Two things should have given the game away here. Firstly, fixed overheads are sunk costs and therefore irrelevant. After all, someone has already committed the business to pay the £9,000 hire of a hanger that accommodates the present six aircraft. Secondly, no matter how tempting it is for an accountant to allocate your 'share' of the hanger costs (one third, or £3,000) there is no element of incremental or opportunity costs at work here! | **Nil** |
| 7. Irrelevant. Depreciation is not a movement of cash; hence it can never score as an incremental or opportunity cost because it never crosses the 'barrier'. Also, what are you doing depreciating this asset: that type of cost is usually rolled up and included in the annual leasing charge made by the owner of the asset. | **Nil** |
| 8. Finally, the leasing charge is, of course, highly relevant. Three times £12,000 gives a total of £36,000. | **–£36,000** |
| **Total result** | **–£340** |

## If the figures don't fit

So what do we make of the idea as a whole? Should we go ahead and lease three further aircraft, or not? The mathematical computation would suggest that we shouldn't. But, for dynamic managers such as ourselves, this is surely just the first 'cut' of this project and we can now go on to fine tune it. Who says that we have included all the potentially relevant revenue and costs; what else should be included? What about the accuracy and sensitivity of some figures? Should we revisit them? This is what happens in real life. We re-examine and re-appraise until we have a solution that suggests with more certainty that we should or shouldn't go ahead.

## Sensitivity analysis

*Key Learning Point*

In this example the result was a narrow fail, so how might we get it to be a pass? We could increase subscriptions, but frankly that isn't going to raise as much money as discontent amongst the members.

We could haggle about the leasing costs, but I doubt whether we could get that moved by more than about 5%, or £600.

The really fruitful area for consideration is the rate per hour charged for flying time. At the moment the contribution is £4 per hour. If we were to raise the selling price per hour charged by £1 to £43 (a small increase of about 2%), we would increase contribution by £1 (a large increase of 25%). This would equate to an increase in revenue of 25% of £30,660, or £7,665. We presumably would be making the increased margin on the other six aircraft too (another £15,330), making an overall increase of £22,995. Now that is worthwhile!

Finally, it is valid to consider other apparently light-hearted things such as gaming machine receipts; often these can tip the balance between viable and non-viable projects.

## Make or buy decisions

Here are two further examples, together with connections that you could be making between the examples and your real world. Firstly, a make or buy decision, then a relocation decision.

Simon Taylor, the purchasing manager of Verygood Valves, recently discovered that the manufacturing cost of B15A units were £7.10 each. He invited two suppliers to tender for making the part externally, and received quotes of £5.00 and £5.40 per unit. Apparently Verygood Valves could make significant savings by purchasing the B15A unit rather than making it.

Before submitting his proposal to the Make/Buy Committee, Simon took another look at the detailed cost sheet, shown below:

| | |
|---|---|
| Labour Cost (20 minutes at £3.00 per hour) | £1.00 |
| Material Cost | £1.10 |
| Manufacturing Overhead | £5.00 |
| *Total Standard Manufacturing Cost per unit* | *£7.10* |

Given that Manufacturing Overhead is 70% fixed and 30% variable, what should Simon recommend?

## Buy

The crucial point to grasp here is that the internally produced apparent cost contains both variable and fixed internal costs. So logically we must ask the question 'If we stop making these B15A units, will the fixed costs actually go away'? By their very nature of being fixed, the answer has to be no. Therefore, they are not relevant costs in helping us arrive at a correct decision in this situation, and we should actually redraft the cost make-up of the product to help us see it in the correct light.

| B15A Units | Total | 30%<br>Variable | 70%<br>Fixed |
|---|---|---|---|
| Labour Costs | £1.00 | £1.00 | |
| Material Costs | £1.10 | £1.10 | |
| Manufacturing Overhead | £5.00 | £1.50 | £3.50 |
| TOTAL | £7.10 | £3.60 | £3.50 |

Since the true variable (incremental or opportunity) cost of making the unit is only £3.60, we would continue to manufacture internally rather than pay outsiders either of the £5.00 or £5.40 per unit quoted. How uncomfortable does all this make you feel about recent decisions that your business may just have made, and about which you and others may well have felt extremely doubtful about at the time?

## Does anyone get it right?

*Key Question*

For example, is a well managed council waste and refuse department actually less cost effective than an outside contractor? How many decisions to 'contract-out' certain bits of operations have been based on flawed costs put into the computational sausage machine: the old 'garbage in, garbage out' syndrome? Alternatively, how many of your businesses are only in existence because of your customers continually making elementary costing mistakes like that above, and giving you the income and profits instead?

Another very useful example to study is this one, which illustrates just how far we have come from the backward looking traditional accounting terms and concepts we had just got used to using. For example, are original cost, depreciation and net book value relevant concepts? See for yourself here.

## A good move?

The problem is that the Hermit Group acquired a ten year lease on a suite of offices in London four years ago, for a cost of £600,000. For financial accounting purposes the net book value (cost less accumulated depreciation) of the lease stood at £360,000 (being £600,000 – (£600,000 x 4/10). The Group was considering moving to the new town of Telford where it was felt that its business could be conducted equally well, and operating savings (excluding lease costs) of about £40,000 per year could be made compared with London. The move itself would cost £20,000. Suitable leasehold premises were available at £400,000 for an initial period of six years. However, the leasehold premises in London could be sub-let for the remaining six years for a sum of only £240,000. Does it make financial sense for the Hermit Group to move?

If we plug in the appropriate figures, we should get the following answer. Note that only cash flows and items that are truly relevant and which relate to future activity have been included.

| Time | Description | Cash flow |
|------|-------------|-----------|
| Now | New lease | -£ 400,000 |
| | Sub lease old | £ 240,000 |
| | Move | -£ 20,000 |
| Year 1 | Savings | £ 40,000 |
| Year 2 | Savings | £ 40,000 |
| Year 3 | Savings | £ 40,000 |
| Year 4 | Savings | £ 40,000 |
| Year 5 | Savings | £ 40,000 |
| Year 6 | Savings | £ 40,000 |
| | | |
| Total cash flows | | £ 60,000 |

From these figures, the total of which are positive, it would appear that the move to Telford is worthwhile. This may be a good example to illustrate the use of sensitivity analysis within financial modelling. Sensitivity analysis simply asks the question, repeatedly and for different constituent costs and revenues, 'By how much will constituent X have to change so that my decision to proceed with the project will actually change to a decision not to proceed?'

To put figures to it, the total annual cost savings of £240,000 (currently £40,000 per annum) would only have to reduce to £180,000 (or £30,000 per annum) for the project not to be worthwhile – and so on. This type of what if, or sensitivity analysis, is being made easier all the time. For example the latest versions of spreadsheets have such tools as 'Scenario Manager' to help you do just this sort of exercise without having to manually manipulate and adjust your data.

# Organisational decision flaws

So, we now know more about the concept of relevant costs in a practical context. Nothing, however, illustrates better just how well the whole thing can blow up than looking at the whole fraught area of profit-centred organisations. To those of you that are in one, you will know what I mean. To those of you who aren't, absorb the following.

## Profit centres

To help set the scene with profit centres, we'd better first describe what they are and what they attempt to achieve. Let's start, then, with the things that aren't profit centres – they're called cost centres, and are the traditional modus operandi of businesses. With a cost centre structure all parts of the business are allocated budgeted amounts that they can spend (costs) in order to support the generation and income of profits for the business as a whole. This is the traditional model – only one department (sales) generates revenue, all other departments generating the opposite (costs). Control is exercised very strictly over all costs incurred, but mainly just the controllable costs will be the responsibility of cost centre managers. Typical performance measures will include traditional variance analyses for cost, volume and efficiency differences.

However, this is often seen in today's business climate (whatever that means!) as being a not too healthy way to run a business. All departments no matter what they do, it is argued, should feel the chill wind of competition and value-for-money. No longer should people be happy just to spend money up to their allocated limits. Instead they should have to compete, drive out inefficiencies and thereby become shining models of efficiency. They are encouraged to do this when management reorganises the business away from the traditional cost-centred structure and into a profit-centred structure.

## Play make-believe

In practice this means that all departments and functions (actually it is rather impractical to do this to all departments, as we will shortly see) now will have to play 'make-believe' that they are wholly independent businesses. They generate income by selling their services internally to other departments within the business (again, only the sales department generates genuine external revenue). Hopefully the income generated will cover their costs and enable them to make a profit for their department, hence the term profit-centre. The theory is that, unless departments provide internal customers with competitive and realistic charges, then the internal customers will look elsewhere for their supplies; and this may well be outside the organisation! All this is supposed to make each department more profit and value-for-money (rather than simply cost) orientated, and the business benefits accordingly. It all sounds fine so far, and in theory it is! The typical performance measure is of course centred on profit and will require control over controllable costs, sales (and transfer) price and output volumes.

(As an aside, there is an intermediate entity called an investment centre. This exercises control over controllable costs, sales and transfer price, output volumes and investment levels. Performance measures are generally based around traditional whole of business financial ratios.)

## Bend the rules to suit

This 'pretend that you're a real independent business' is decidedly interesting to the managers involved, as invariably a sizeable proportion of their pay may now be made performance (or profit) related. Actual performance, in the new language of 'profitspeak', becomes all-important; which is actually what the whole system was designed to do in the first place. So, everyone's happy, and off we all go to build a world-class business? Well, it isn't quite like that. Indeed the reality of daily life within a profit centred organisation can be so far from what the initial intentions were in the first place that, after two or three years of total anarchy (and reduced corporate profitability), the whole idea is given up. Back we go to cost centres! This scenario of giving up profit centred structures is becoming more and more commonplace. Let's see why.

Essentially the fundamental principle as to why profit centres should work is, of course, good. What stands in the way of transferring theory into practice is, as always, people's stupidity. Here is a brief real life example.

This computer peripherals company decided to profit centre their business. Of relevance to us today are really only two parts of the business – the factory in Eire, and the sales operation based in the UK. As you would no doubt guess, the factory 'sold' its production to the sales force, which then in turn sold it to the real outside world of customers. You can't get much simpler than that.

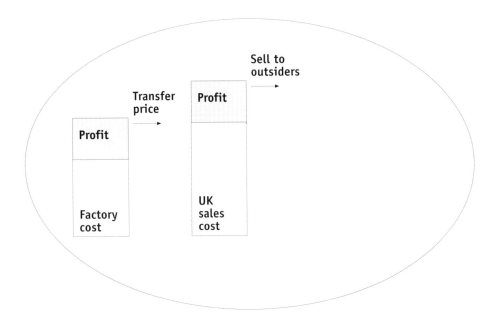

## Transfer prices

Now we need to introduce the cornerstone of profit-centred organisations, and it's a concept I have kept deliberately hidden so far, it's called the 'Transfer Price'. It works like this. In order to play this game of 'pretending' to be real businesses within the one real business, management only has to play just one interfering part. That is in setting the price at which goods and services will be sold and bought at each stage from one profit centre to another; this is the 'Transfer Price'. It does of course make a great deal of good sense for this to be set in advance, so that all parties know how much to include in their budgets, and so on.

So, in the context of the example described, the factory manager would be told to get on with production. Since his transfer price across to the UK Sales department is known, the factory manager will be incentivised along the lines of 'You can keep 10% of any additional profit made above 10% net'. He is

*Key Management Concept*

therefore keenly interested in driving down his costs to make more profit and hence personal gain (he can't do anything with his selling price, since it is fixed – the transfer price).

The sales department doesn't give a hoot as to what is actually going on within the factory, since their buying-in price is fixed – the transfer price. All sales have to do is to keep making sales.

## The wasted debate

So everyone in the business is happy, until one day the factory manager realises that if he could increase the transfer price he could make himself some more money. Coincidentally, the sales manager has been thinking lately that the transfer price in to him from the factory is too high, he simply cannot make his targets, and hence his personal profit share targets. They both decide to convene a meeting about the transfer price as soon as possible, and set their subordinates many tasks to dig out supporting information for their respective causes. A meeting duly takes place at which there is a bitter row, and working parties are instigated to review the matter further.

## Profit centre decay

*Key Question*

Organisations become obsessed with the transfer price, to the extent that corporate time, expertise and resource is squandered on the greatest non-debate in the civilised world. Just ask this one question: 'Does the organisation as a whole generate more profits if a particular transfer price is set higher or lower?' And the answer is, of course, a resounding 'No'. Debating the transfer price doesn't make a jot of difference to the business overall. You do have to admit, though, that it might make manager X richer than manager Y, but that is hardly the point of the whole initiative, is it? So there we have it, a business generally degenerates into squabbles about transfer pricing and turf wars, all to the detriment of the greater corporate health.

## Directors as referees

One of the ways to prevent this is to ensure that senior management (the main board) understand that, with the advent of a profit centred structure, they have to add an additional skill to their quiver, that of refereeing and arbitrating. Firm management of transfer pricing is essential; most switched-on businesses will allow all of one hour of debate per annum on it, and that's it.

But that actually isn't the worst problem with profit centres, not by a long chalk. There is actually a more insidious creeping affliction that is not often noticed until it's too late to do anything about it. It's known as the phenomenon of 'Ritual Sacrifice'. We've all seen examples of it, the slow bleeding to death of perfectly good internal departments and operations on the altar of lowest possible cost when compared unfavourably to external providers. The former Public Sector has been particularly efficient at developing expertise in this dark art.

## Profit centre disaster 1

Here is how it happens, and I will give you two examples. The first one you will say couldn't possibly happen in a sensible business. But then when we look at the second, you will nod your heads in despair as you recognise the same thing that happened in your business.

For the first example we will simply extend the computer peripheral company, since it actually happened there. We will need to extend the diagram as well, this time to include a third area of operation glamorously known as European sales. Now the European sales function had to buy all of its goods for resale from UK sales at a transfer price. This transfer price was actually quite high by now. After all, the UK sales department didn't actually want to sell things at anything less than full market price. When they could sell all they wanted to domestically and make good profits, why should they do European sales a favour and sell to them at a discount? Sadly, for the Europeans, they then found that they couldn't actually sell anything in Europe for more than the transfer price – it was simply prohibitively high.

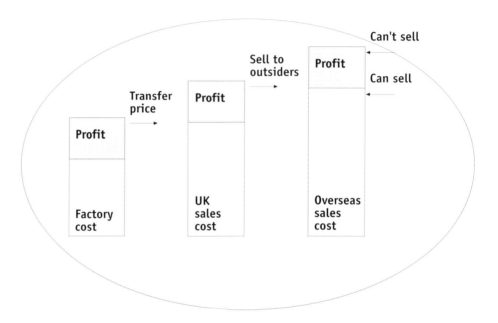

So what do you think that the European sales department did? Go direct to the factory? A sensible option, you might think, and one that would probably get endorsed by the main board. No, instead they bought the goods in from a competitor.

Now although you might find this amazingly foolish, simply put yourself in the shoes of the European sales department. As far as you are aware, you are required to make as much profit as you can. Selling the internally produced items is getting you absolutely nowhere, in profit terms, so something has to be done. The bulk purchase deal from a competitor seemed too good to miss, and doing this will enable you to meet your profit targets. But, why is everyone so upset with you?

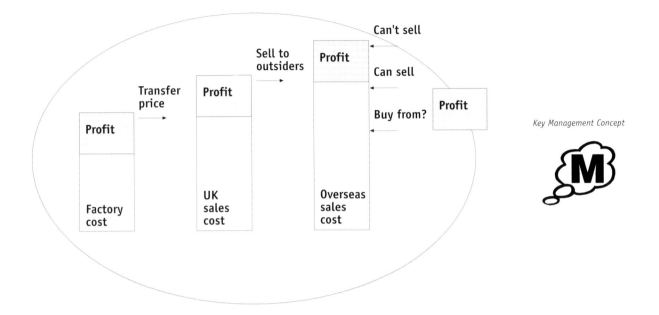

*Key Management Concept*

Well it's obvious really, isn't it? The transfer price/profit centre structure conspires against any one centre being able to make decisions for the good of the whole business. A decision that is good for the local profit centre will always win out against a better decision for the whole business – always. That is the risk you took in the first place in instituting a profit centre regime!

## Profit centre disaster 2

The second example is one altogether much closer to home. Imagine one of the more obscure profit centres in a business; I like to think of Training, a subject close to my heart. Every year your Training Department publishes a Training Directory, although this year (the first as profit centres) you discover that there is a price alongside each programme. You are somewhat astonished at the price that is being charged, especially as training costs now come out of your own profits!

You have ten employees that you want to attend a time management course. Your own Training Department want to charge £200 per delegate per day, making a total of £2,000. By the time you have added on travel to the National Training Centre the total cost will be nearer £3,000. As luck would have it one of your dinner guests runs their own training business, and offers you a local programme in your office for £100 per delegate per day, or a total of £1,000. Now, which one of the options do you prefer? How long will it take you to decide? Of course you opt for the local external provider.

Well, actually, perhaps you shouldn't, but it does depend whether you are wearing a local profit centre hat or a whole-of-business hat. Just imagine if most other profit centres in the business were also making similar decisions about training. Poor old Training Department; they suddenly aren't getting any business. They are not making profits so they have to cut costs (sack people) and put prices up. The inevitable happens, and the Department goes to the wall. 'They were just too expensive', and 'They lost their best people, we just lost faith in them' are epitaphs that could equally well appear on many tombstones of the recently departed.

## One inevitable conclusion

The real problem is that they didn't have a chance of fighting back. Unless management is extremely vigilant, almost any function can be lost in a similar way. A more powerful argument against this happening is this one. Try making your profit centres pay for goods and services internally in rubber bands, paper clips, chocolate buttons – anything but real money. Do you remember the debate we had in an earlier part which said that anything internal was not a relevant cost? Do you also remember the debate we have only just finished about the unreality of transfer prices? Why then do businesses continue to equate an internal pound with an external pound?

## Payment in paper clips, please

The pound paid to your Training Department is not really a pound at all. If it makes you feel any happier you can believe it is a pound, but it isn't really. The pound is still within the organisation as a whole, and that's what counts. Contrast that with the situation where you have paid a pound to an external provider – that pound is real, it is part of cash flow, and once paid it has gone from the organisation forever. That is real money.

As for the scope of this problem, well this happens not just to my hypothetical Training Department. It can happen to just about anyone in a business: IT, Distribution and Logistics, Facilities Maintenance, Printing and (recently) Finance.

## Pros and cons of profit centres

To summarise let's look at a simple list of the pros and cons of being a profit centre.

The two main advantages are:

- It emphasises the 'bottom line', motivates managers to perform well in areas they control, and encourages initiatives.
- It gives local managers responsibility and helps to train top managers of the future, thereby freeing top management time.

*Key Management Concept*

The two main disadvantages are:

- The eternal transfer price problems, confusion of centre's result with manager's performance, and possible over-emphasis on short-term results.
- Profit centres may make mistakes which top managers might avoid, thereby under-utilising corporate competence and duplication of activities.

## Terminal decay

Finally, in tabular form, an illustration as to how badly things can go wrong. Here are two factories which produce pens. 'A' only makes blue pens, whilst 'B' makes many different colours. The nub of the problem is of course how should 'B' allocate the (obviously greater) costs of producing different colour pens between each colour. If he does this allocation equally, to 'B' it will appear that blue pens cost more to make than 'A' thinks.

|  | Factory A | Factory B |
|---|---|---|
| **Produces** | 1 million blue pens | 1 million pens, all colours |
| **Costs** | Low | High |
| **Price leader?** | Yes | No |
| **Allocates costs** | All to the blue pens | Equally between all different coloured pens |
| **Relative costs** | N/A – only one product is being made | Blues appear to be dearer to produce than at factory A |
| **Action** | N/A – none needed | Stops producing blue pens |
| **Outcome** | Sells more blues, as B's blue pens are expensive | Other pens get dearer, as costs have not actually gone away |
| **Final result** | Takes over B | Goes out of business |
| **Moral** | Other people are stupid | Get costs right the first time |

# Computing
# future decisions

# Chapter 7

# Dealing with the future

So we've looked at costs for decision-making and we've come up with our list of golden rules. This list isn't exactly earth shattering, but if you've stuck with the discussion above, you can see that the practical problems which businesses encounter in everyday life can be immense. Oddly enough the situation in this management accounting arena (few rules, much confusion) seems to be diametrically opposed to that of the financial accounting arena (many rules, less confusion).

Now you might have spotted already that the way in which we have made decisions has been, some people would say, a little too simplistic and one-dimensional. I would have to agree to some extent, and this is the area we are about to explore now. We will add another dimension to our decision-making, the dimension of time.

## A more scientific approach

Take the following example. A business reckons that if it spends £1,000 on a new machine, then it can generate net revenues of £400 per annum for the next three years. The machine at the end of three years will have no value. Do you think that the business should undertake the project?

*Key Question*

To help us decide a project's viability we need a measure to judge it by. What is the simplest measure of overall financial benefit? How about simply adding the sums together and calculating the net result. If we do this we get the sum of £200, indicating that the project may well be worthwhile. Perhaps it would be better if we were to express the problem diagrammatically.

| Time | Item | Amount |
|------|------|--------|
| 0 | Purchase of new machine | -£ 1,000 |
| 1 | Net revenue | £ 400 |
| 2 | Net revenue | £ 400 |
| 3 | Net revenue | £ 400 |
| | Net result | £ 200 |

## Conventions

Note the accepted conventions at work here:

- The first column indicates the time, with time '0' taken as being now, time 1 being one year from now and so on

- It is assumed that all items arise at the end of the year. This may not be very realistic, but actually those who model on a monthly basis don't find a great deal of difference overall.

- All we count is real opportunity costs, which generally means net cash hence the heading 'cash flows'.

## Accounting rate of return

So, what do we think? We get a net benefit of £200, or 20% return on the investment. Hold on a minute, though, that return has been made over three years, so the annualised return is more like just over 6%. Now that doesn't seem too good, especially as the rate we could have got by sticking the initial investment in the bank might well be at least that return. And, of course, any project must have risk, and our business has risk too! It looks marginal, but still positive.

*Key Management Concept*

Here is the beginning of a list of measures that are commonly used by all businesses, and we have just looked at the commonest one of all: the accounting rate of return (or profitability). Although we have calculated a simple return and annualised it, strictly the accounting rate of return is calculated as the average annual accounting profit divided by the average capital employed; not so very far from the all-powerful 'Return on capital employed', or ROCE.

The advantages of the accounting rate of return are that it is quick and easy to calculate, easy to understand and ends up with a familiar percentage figure. The disadvantages are that there are no set rules for determining minimum acceptable return; definitions of capital employed and profits are often unclear; and it uses accounting profit rather than cash as a measure of benefit.

## An alternative scenario

Let's see how this simplest measure deals with a modified example, one that we as sophisticated people will grasp instinctively. Let us assume that, instead of the original equal cash flows of £400 per annum, we now get annual cash flows of £nil, £800 and £400. What do we think about the project now, using this measure?

| Time | Item | Amount | Modified |
|---|---|---|---|
| 0 | Purchase of new machine | -£ 1,000 | -£1,000 |
| 1 | Net revenue | £ 400 | £0 |
| 2 | Net revenue | £ 400 | £800 |
| 3 | Net revenue | £ 400 | £400 |
| | Net result | £ 200 | £ 200 |

The answer is that the return is identical to that seen previously, and yet instinctively the former scenario simply looks much better than the latter. Why? Because the cash revenues arise earlier in the original than the modified example, and our gut-feeling tells us that this is better. Accounting rate of return therefore ignores timing and time value of money.

# Payback period

Travelling along the road of financial sophistication, we come to the concept known as 'Payback'. Payback is the time (cumulative) taken to recoup the initial investment. Look back to the original example, what is its payback period? The answer is two and a half years. After one year we have recouped £400, after two years it is a cumulative £800, and after three years it is a cumulative £1,200. We pass the cumulative £1,000 therefore in the 'middle' of year three – hence a payback of two and a half years.

## Payback norms

What are generally accepted benchmarks for a payback period? You may well hear in your organisation an 'etched in stone' dictat such as 'We will only undertake a project if it pays back within two years'. Now there's nothing magical about two years, just as there isn't about three, or four or five years. Instead, the choice of acceptable payback periods is entirely up to each individual business. All it does reveal is how the business regards its cash flow, as effectively that is what payback is a measure of; how quickly will we get our initial investment back. It says nothing about profitability or future medium and long-term viability. A business will very often shorten its minimum acceptable payback period when times are hard (especially on the cash flow front), perhaps even to a period of less than a year. Contrast that with the big capital spenders such as the cable companies and National Grid, who are happy to have payback periods of several years or more, such is the nature of their business.

## A cash flow measure?

In summary, payback concentrates on how rapidly a project pays back its own outlay. It is based on profit, or cash flow. Its advantages are that it is quick and easy to calculate, easy to understand, and it emphasises speed of return (important when liquidity problems loom). Its disadvantages are that there are no set rules for payback period times and it ignores cash flows outside the payback period. Payback is therefore a very blunt and subjective tool, and yet the vast majority of businesses are happy to appraise projects that will determine whether that business ultimately succeeds or fails simply on the back of this measure.

To see how potentially disappointing payback can be, what is the payback period in the modified example? The answer is still two and a half years. So, payback also fails to discriminate between the two projects, the original and the modified, and hence the time value of money. There has to be a better way to measure projects – at least better than accounting return or payback. There is a measure, and the reason it is better is that it incorporates what the previous two have studiously ignored, what is known in the trade as the 'time value of money'. Just before that, though, let us now briefly summarise some of the key (not including discounted cash flow) decision rules.

## Single independent project

In payback terms the project must generate profits/cash flows to pay back the required outlay with a maximum specified time period. In accounting return terms the project must generate ROCE greater than some minimum acceptable ROCE.

## Mutually exclusive projects

In payback terms first select the project which pays back its initial outlay quickest, then check to see if this project pays back its outlay within the maximum specified time period. In accounting return terms first select the project with highest ROCE; then check to see if this project has an ROCE greater than or equal to, some minimum acceptable ROCE.

# Time value of money

Back to our time value of money debate, and before we examine the 'better way' we need to establish exactly what is meant by the 'time value of money'. After all, in our accounting return and payback models we have gaily been adding future cash flows together. But surely this is madness? A pound at time 1 (an apple) is not equal to a pound at time 2 (a pear) is not equal to a pound at time 3 (a banana) and so on. We were guilty of producing a fruit salad when we were looking at the accounting return and payback computations!

*Key Management Concept*

## Present values

Let us take a simple example. I offer to give you £1 in exactly one year's time. You thank me very much, but you can't really be bothered to wait for a whole year. You would rather have the money now, but since I am hardly likely to give you the full £1 now I will presumably offer you a lesser amount! Here's how we work it out. What sum now plus one year's worth of interest on that sum will exactly equal £1 in one year? Assuming that the rate of interest available is about 10%, what plus 10% equals £1 in one year? The mathematical answer is approximately £0.91 (check it to see: 91p plus 9.1p does just about equal £1). We could take it back one further year; what is the value today of 91p in one year's time? The answer is about 83p (83p plus 8.3p is approximately 91p).

## Discounting

This stupefyingly simple principle is the key that unlocks one of life's great puzzles: how to add together future sums of money. The principle is called 'discounting'; in other words we are discounting a future sum back to a value today, also know as the 'present value'. Do these terms sound familiar from those boardroom discussions of the past?

What you have just calculated is the beginning of what is known as a 'discount table'. Below are the discount tables for 10% and 20% rates of interest. What relationship do they bear to one another?

| Time | 10% | 20% |
|------|------|------|
| 0 | 1.00 | 1.00 |
| 1 | 0.91 | 0.83 |
| 2 | 0.83 | 0.69 |
| 3 | 0.75 | 0.58 |
| 4 | 0.68 | 0.48 |
| 5 | 0.62 | 0.40 |
| 6 | 0.56 | 0.33 |
| 7 | 0.51 | 0.28 |
| 8 | 0.47 | 0.23 |
| 9 | 0.42 | 0.19 |
| 10 | 0.39 | 0.16 |
| 1-10 inclusive | 6.14 | 4.17 |

## Future values, or compounding

Now for those of you with endowment mortgages this indeed makes grim reading. Do you remember one of the hooks you were put out to dry on was the one about the terminal bonus? 'How would you like a terminal bonus of £30,000 at the end of your 25 year mortgage Mr. Smith?' Your mind immediately thought of the shiny BMW or 30' yacht – but wait. What do you suppose is the discount factor for time 25 at 10%? Do you really want to know? It is about 0.08, which means that instead of offering you a terminal bonus of £30,000 perhaps they should have said 'the equivalent of £2,400 (being £30,000 times 0.08) in today's terms'. That's not much of your BMW or a yacht now, is it? Ah, the tricks we all play with the time value of money!

## Inflation plays no part

One key thing to understand now is that this whole principle has absolutely nothing to do with inflation (which is the amount by which prices increase in nominal terms). What discounting does is to show the present value of amounts receivable (or payable) at some time in the future. Some large organisations believe that inflation must be built in to the financial model, but don't believe them. Factoring – in inflation rarely makes a significant difference to the decision outcome.

So, let's try and make sense of all this with our earlier example.

| Time | Item | Amount |
|---|---|---|
| 0 | Purchase of new machine | -£ 1,000 |
| 1 | Net revenue | £ 400 |
| 2 | Net revenue | £ 400 |
| 3 | Net revenue | £ 400 |
| | Net result | £ 200 |

# Discounted cash flow

We now need to add another column that will show the discount factor, like this. I will assume a 10% factor.

| Time | Item | Amount | 10% discount factor |
|------|------|--------|---------------------|
| 0 | Purchase of new machine | -£ 1,000 | 1.00 |
| 1 | Net revenue | £ 400 | 0.91 |
| 2 | Net revenue | £ 400 | 0.83 |
| 3 | Net revenue | £ 400 | 0.75 |
| | Net result | £ 200 | |

We then need to cross-multiply the amount of the cash flow by the discount factor, and what we get is the discounted cash flow, or DCF. This is then added down to give the sum of all the discounted cash flows, often called the net present value, or NPV.

| Time | Item | Amount | 10% discount factor | Discounted cash flow |
|------|------|--------|---------------------|----------------------|
| 0 | Purchase of new machine | -£ 1,000 | 1.00 | -£1,000 |
| 1 | Net revenue | £ 400 | 0.91 | £364 |
| 2 | Net revenue | £ 400 | 0.83 | £332 |
| 3 | Net revenue | £ 400 | 0.75 | £300 |
| | Net result | £ 200 | NPV = | -£ 4 |

## Net present value

So what does a net present value actually mean, and what is the relevance of this particular answer of minus £4? Well they are really only three things to consider when trying to interpret the meaning. Firstly we have an initial investment, secondly a discount rate, and thirdly a resultant net present value. If we put all these three things together to try to explain the concept, this is what we might say. 'If we were to invest £1,000 in this project, and the cost of borrowing that sum was 10% interest, then at the end of the project we would be £4 worse off than we would be if we did absolutely nothing'. How does that sound?

Alternatively, we could say that doing this project leaves us £4 worse off than had we put £1,000 in the bank at 10% interest. Whatever slant we take, it doesn't look like this project is going to be worthwhile. But that's another issue, isn't it? Who says (and why and how) what an acceptable return is? We will discuss this later, after a little more manipulation of the example, but the general conclusion is that we are prepared to do anything that has a positive net present value.

## Effect of discount rate

The result of the same example but now with a discount rate of 12% is interesting. Is it more or less worthwhile?

| Time | Item | Amount | 12% discount factor | Discounted cash flow |
|---|---|---|---|---|
| 0 | Purchase of new machine | -£ 1,000 | 1.00 | -£1,000 |
| 1 | Net revenue | £ 400 | 0.89 | £357 |
| 2 | Net revenue | £ 400 | 0.80 | £319 |
| 3 | Net revenue | £ 400 | 0.71 | £285 |
| | Net result | £ 200 | NPV = | -£ 39 |

Since the net present value has decreased from negative £4 to negative £39, the project is even less worthwhile. Using a higher discount rate therefore makes future cash flows less attractive, and the project appear less viable.

Likewise, the result of the same example but now with a discount rate of 8% is interesting. Is it more or less worthwhile?

| Time | Item | Amount | 8% discount factor | Discounted cash flow |
|---|---|---|---|---|
| 0 | Purchase of new machine | -£ 1,000 | 1.00 | -£1,000 |
| 1 | Net revenue | £ 400 | 0.93 | £370 |
| 2 | Net revenue | £ 400 | 0.86 | £343 |
| 3 | Net revenue | £ 400 | 0.79 | £318 |
| | Net result | £ 200 | NPV = | £ 31 |

Since the net present value has increased from negative £4 to positive £31, the project is more worthwhile. Using a lower discount rate therefore makes future cash flows more attractive, and the project appear more viable.

## Internal rate of return

There will be a point (i.e. discount rate) for a project where the net present value is £nil. For this project that point would be a rate of just less than 10%; say about 9.7%. This discount rate (the rate that gives a net present value of £nil) is called the 'Internal Rate of Return', or IRR.

## IRR and NPV together

This concept of IRR is indeed a sister concept to that of NPV and the two tend to be viewed together. Typical criteria for acceptance are:

- **NPV** – do if positive

- **IRR** – do if rate is greater than can be achieved elsewhere.

Businesses tend to set their yardsticks like this. A positive NPV means that the business will not go down the pan, but the IRR is still used to give a feel for the 'profitability' (please note that it isn't actually profitability at all, and we should really be careful not to call it that).

## Summary of criteria

So our now refined list of decision-making criteria is:

1. Accounting rate of return

2. Payback period

3. Discounted cash flow: NPV and IRR

Of these three, the only real heavyweight one is the discounted cash flow. Having spent some time describing what it is and how it is used, let us now test its difficulties – and there are three significant problems. These are interest rate, time scale and accuracy.

## Interest rate

Continuing where we left off discussing IRR, you can see that the choice of an appropriate interest rate is critical; the interest rate will radically alter the project's perceived assessment. So what do we use as a rate, and how do we decide? Essentially there are three things to weigh up in making that decision:

1. Marginal

2. WACC and

3. Hurdle Rates.

## Marginal

Firstly, what is the actual cost of borrowing the money that is being used to fund the project? This is known as the marginal or actual rate, and it doesn't take a genius to see that there is little point in pursuing a project if its costs are greater than its returns.

## Weighted

Secondly what is the weighted average cost of capital, or WACC? WACC is the average rate of interest a business pays on all its funding sources, from debt and borrowings through to equity finance. An example of WACC might help. Assume that a business has a debt to equity ratio of 3 to 1 (three pounds of borrowed money for every pound of shareholder's money), not an uncommon figure for a successful business. The cost of equity finance is, nominally, the dividend yield we looked at in an earlier section. This is around 4% for the FTSE All Share index (most people would dispute this and say that the cost of equity is substantially higher than the cost of debt, but let's just stick to the basics here). The cost of debt finance has, in the recent past, averaged out at around 12%. We can draw up a simple relationship like this to illustrate the figures.

|  | Capital structure | Cost of money | Weighted cost |
|---|---|---|---|
| Equity | £ 1 | 4% | £ 0.04 |
| Debt | £ 3 | 12% | £ 0.36 |
| Total | £ 4 | | £ 0.40 |

The weighted average cost of capital is therefore the cost of financing (£0.40) divided by the capital (£4.00) or 10%. Isn't it amazing just how often answers come out to be good old 10%; handy too since it's a nice round number. The problem is that because it's such an easy figure it has been adopted by most businesses as the only rate that is ever used for discounting and NPV calculations, and as we have already seen that might simply not be correct.

As a contrast, in Japan even now the interest rates are so low that they might consider this project hugely worthwhile. Because we use a rate of interest that is high compared to other countries and cultures, we are in danger of rejecting projects that the others will only too gladly take up. What nationality is it that is backing massive inward investment such as cars, high technology manufacturing and cable companies? It isn't UK money, due to our perceived high cost of capital.

## Hurdle or premium

The third consideration to take into account in establishing an appropriate discount rate is what is often known as a Hurdle rate. This isn't as complex as it may sound, all it means is that we will add a rate premium to a normal discount rate, to reflect the risk of a project. For example, a project which is 'core' or fundamental to a business may be discounted at 10%, but if that business were appraising a project to diversify into, say, estate agency, the discount rate may be increased to reflect the greater risk of the project. After all, the business has no track record, expertise, management and so on in the new venture – so it is risky. Hurdle rates such as 20% or even 25% are not unknown for non-core projects; if the project works, even at such a high discount rate, then we may well be prepared to do it.

## Time scale

Our discounted cash flow worked example showed a net present value of minus £4. What, however, would our view of the project have been had the cash inflows lasted for just one more year? The answer is that we would have looked altogether more favourably upon the idea, and may well have decided to go ahead. Here are the figures:

| Item | Amount | 10% discount factor | Discounted cash flow |
|------|--------|--------------------|---------------------|
| Purchase of new machine | -£ 1,000 | 1.00 | -£1,000 |
| Net revenue | £ 400 | 0.91 | £364 |
| Net revenue | £ 400 | 0.83 | £332 |
| Net revenue | £ 400 | 0.75 | £300 |
| Net revenue | £ 400 | 0.68 | £272 |
| Net result | £ 600 | NPV = | £ 268 |

The NPV has increased from minus £4 to positive £268, a significant turnaround. Also, the IRR has moved from just below 10% to around 22%, altogether much more worthwhile. The point I'm trying to get at here is not so much whether it's worth doing or not, but rather the impact that simply adding an extra year can have on the overall viability. Who is to say that this project will only last for three years – why not four? We now get to the unenviable situation where you can practically justify anything if you are prepared to go far enough in extending/bending assumptions. Some people are very good at this; I have seen blue chip PLC's with project appraisal plans lasting for twelve years or more. They probably won't even be in business in twelve years time! It all becomes, if not properly controlled, a futile exercise in self-justification: 'I am going to do this project, so I'd better make the figures look good' type of thing.

# Accuracy

Continuing along from the last point about self-justification, the purported accuracy of some business's cash flows is stunning. To say that in year eight the overall cash flow will be say, £12,689,994, is obviously unrealistic. And yet businesses carry on with this myth that accuracy is all-important. Two (or perhaps three at a push) significant figures would be sufficient. This would give a more realistic £13,000,000, or £12,700,000.

Those, then, are the three key items on which the outcome of a discounted cash flow computation is likely to be dependent. Two further words of warning are necessary here, though.

## Final pleas

Firstly, please don't forget that the cash flows you are discounting (and hence the answer you get) are only going to be as good as the accuracy of the relevant (opportunity, incremental) costs that you have identified in the first place. If there is any inaccuracy in a computation it is less likely to be in the NPV/IRR computation (after all, a spreadsheet will take care of this) than in what you are counting as relevant in the first place.

Secondly, a word about the overall behaviour patterns in making financial decisions. You may well have encountered the following model on learning at almost any stage of you career. It is relevant to so many situations, and it is easy to remember and describe.

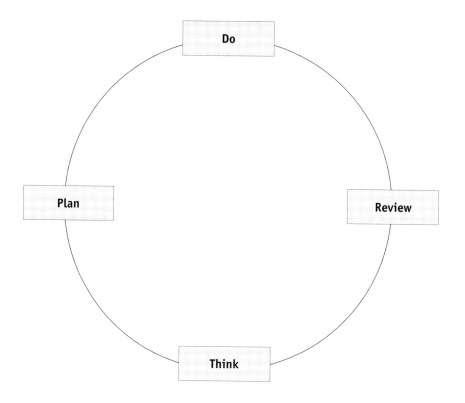

## Learning cycle

This learning cycle can be described in a simple example. You put your hand near a fire (do), and of course it gets hot. You decide that the act of putting it near a fire made it hot (review). That means that all fires are hot (think), so you decide to avoid getting too close to fires in the future (plan). The point behind this learning model is that unless you go through all four stages in the right order, then it is unlikely that you are learning anything.

## Plan, do, review, think – or do we?

When you apply the concept to finance in general; and to decision making in particular, you find that it is entirely relevant. Accountants are very good at the plan and do stages, but not good at the review and think parts. Cast your mind back to your own annual internal budgeting charade. It happens every year in the same way and the same devices and untruths are trotted out, it's like the organisation learns nothing from last year's debacle. Well, the same holds true for decision-making. We spend a lot of time on the planning (DCF, NPV, IRR and so on) and then the actual doing, but very little (if any) time is spent on the review and thinking stages after the event. As a result many businesses are (and have been for many years) undertaking projects that in real life are rubbish. Incredibly few businesses, it seems, really want to know a cold hard assessment as to whether the supposed benefits that we were told a project would bring have actually been delivered. The learning model says that until you do exactly that, then your business hasn't learned anything!

# Comprehensive example

*Activity*

Now that we have explored the assumptions and draw backs of the model, we will finish off project appraisal with a slightly more complex example. Here it is.

Producer Limited has recently bought a new factory in Southampton for £750,000 and is now considering equiping it with either new or second hand plant.

New plant would cost £300,000; the alternative is to transfer old plant from an existing factory in Manchester. This old plant was bought two years ago for £250,000 and now has a book value of £140,625. The old plant has the same capacity as the new £300,000 plant, but being of a slightly different design, would cost £200,000 to replace in the existing factory in Manchester if it was decided to make use of the old plant in the new factory. The old plant has a current market value of £100,000 and would require £50,000 to enable it to be moved to its new location and have the same life as the new machinery. The new Southampton factory, bought at a bargain 'never to be repeated' price, has a current market value of £800,000.

All machinery has a life of 10 years during which time it could generate net cash inflows of £120,000 per annum. At the end of the 10 years all machinery would have negligible scrap value. The factory, with an anticipated useful life of 45 years, would have a market value of £550,000 in 10 years time.

Ignoring tax and inflation you are required to:

a) Decide on the best method of equipping the new factory, and

b) Decide whether or not it is worth equipping the new factory.

Assume a cost of capital of 10%.

## Solution

Notice that the question is versed in a kind and helpful way; answer part a) before attempting to answer part b). Just think about the reality of the situation. In real life decisions are not just simple do/don't do switches, they are made up of many separate sub-decisions and assumptions that all roll-up into a final overall decision. The technique to get this right is often known as the 'decision tree' model, where sub-decisions are taken sequentially and logically, all rolling up into a final overall decision (which is the subject of the DCF calculation). Decision trees look like this, and we have put the decision as to the best method of equiping the new factory on one branch, which will then roll up into the decision as to whether or not it is worth equiping the new factory at all.

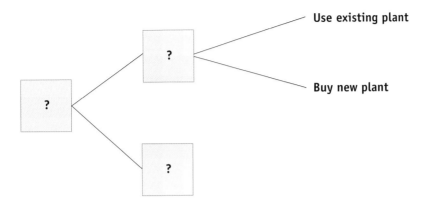

You can see from the diagram that, before we decide whether to go ahead with the overall venture, we need to decide what the lower cost option is of getting plant in place. All we need to do is to put the relevant figures into place. The cost as a whole to the organisation of new plant is £300,000. The cost of using the existing plant is the £50,000 moving costs and the £200,000 needed to replace the old plant in Manchester. Which is lower £300,000 or £250,000? Obviously the latter, so £250,000 is the answer to this decision point and we can put this figure in at the decision node.

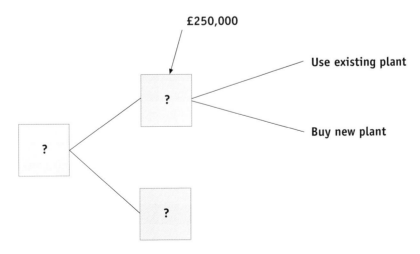

Now we can proceed with the final DCF calculation. The only real way to get this right is to ensure that we have the right relevant costs in the first place. And the only way to get the relevant costs right is to use the three column approach here. One column represents the costs if the project is undertaken, the second represents the costs if the project is rejected, whilst the third is the difference between columns one and two.

| Time | Item | A Cash flows if project accepted | B Cash flows if project rejected | A-B Cash flow differences |
|---|---|---|---|---|
| 0 | | | | |
| 1 | | | | |
| 2 | | | | |
| 3 | | | | |
| 4 | | | | |

If we are now to put the figures in to the proforma, the result will look like this:

| Time | Item | A Cash flows if project accepted | B Cash flows if project rejected | A-B Cash flow differences | 10% Discount factor | Discounted Cash Flows |
|---|---|---|---|---|---|---|
| 0 | Plant/Sale of factory | -£ 250 | 800 | -£ 1,050 | 1.00 | -£1,050 |
| 1 to 10 | Net revenue | £ 120 | | £ 120 | 6.14 | £737 |
| 10 | Proceeds of site | £ 550 | | £ 550 | 0.39 | £215 |
| | | | | | NPV | -£99 |

Whilst the first column looks fairly self-explanatory (purchase of plant, net revenue for ten years, sale of site after ten years), we had better explain the second column. What you have to bear in mind is what would the business do if the project were not to go ahead? Sell the factory site, obviously.

The net result (A-B) gives the cash flow differences or relevant cash flows, ready for discounting. Rather than write out the flows for years 1 to 10, we have used a shorthand version. This is because, mathematically, discounting £120 for each of the ten years gives the same answer as multiplying £120 once by the 'cumulative' discount factor of 6.14. Look back at the discount tables earlier in this chapter to see that 6.14 is simply the sum of the individual factors from 1 to 10 (i.e. 0.91 plus 0.83 plus 0.75 and so on).

Finally we can see the result of the discounted cash flow computation, a negative £99. Obviously it is not worth doing.

# Final thoughts

So, this is the end of our journey through the maze of finance, accounting and scorekeeping. I hope that as a result of reading this book you will be a more financially confident and questioning person in the future. Remember, finance is the most important thing in business.

# Hawksmere information

## Hawksmere – quality programmes and practical value

Hawksmere is one of the UK s leading training organisations, providing high quality programmes allied to practical value. Every year we present around 450 public seminars as well as working with clients on a comprehensive range of in-company tailored training.

## Our objective for each delegate

Our aim at every course is to provide each participant with added expertise, techniques and ideas of practical use. Our speakers are practitioners who are pre-eminent in their own field: as a result, the information and advice on offer are both expert and tried and tested.

## Hawksmere offers you a broad in-depth range, from skills to strategies

Our programmes cover a wide range from management development to law, finance, insurance, government contracts and project management. They span all levels, from introductory skills to sophisticated techniques and the implications of complex legislation.

## A continuing search for improvement

Our policy is to continue to re-examine and develop our successful courses, constantly updating and improving them. We offer a mixed range of one and two day public programmes, combined with some longer residential courses.

Our aim is to continue to anticipate the shifting, often complex challenges facing everyone in both the professions and industry, and to provide programmes of high quality, focused on producing practical results.

For further information on all our public seminars, call our Sales Department on 0171 824 8257.

## Hawksmere In-Company

Hawksmere trainers are all professionals with sound practical experience. Our approach is participative, with extensive use of case studies and group work. The emphasis is on working with clients to define objectives, develop content and deliver in the appropriate way. This gives our client total our client involvement and support are prime contributors to the success of any programme.

As with our public seminars, participants in Hawksmere In-Company programmes will receive a customised course manual produced to our own high standard which will serve as useful reference documentation after the course.

## What can we offer you?

We can provide training in all the areas covered by our public seminar programmes as well as in other topics which you may identify. In summary we can offer you:

- Tailored company programmes producing real results.

- Expert speakers matched to your company profile.

- Flexibility of time and place.

- Maximum impact on productivity through training your staff at a pace to suit you.

- Your total control over course content.

- Advice on the training needs of individuals.